On Core
Mathematics

Kindergarten

HOUGHTON MIFFLIN HARCOURT

Cover photo credit: maxstock/Alamy

Printed in the U.S.A.

ISBN 978-0-547-57521-6

13 0928 20 19 18 17 16 15 14

4500480554   ^ B C D E F G

Table of Contents

Counting and Cardinality

▶ **Know number names and the count sequence.**

▶ **Count to tell the number of objects.**

▶ **Compare numbers.**

Operations and Algebraic Thinking

▶ Understand addition as putting together and adding to, and understand subtraction as taking apart and taking from.

Number and Operations in Base Ten

▶ Work with numbers 11–19 to gain foundations for place value.

Measurement and Data

▶ Describe and compare measurable attributes.

▶ Classify objects and count the number of objects in each category.

Geometry

Lesson 1

COMMON CORE STANDARD CC.K.CC.1

Lesson Objective: Know the count
sequence when counting to 50 by ones.

Count to 50 by Ones

1	2	3	4	5	6	7	8	9	10
11	12	13	14	15	16	17	18	19	20
21	22	23	24	25	26	27	28	29	30
31	32	33	34	35	36	37	38	39	40
41	42	43	44	45	46	47	48	49	50

DIRECTIONS 1. Count forward from 1. Draw a dot on each number as you
count. Begin with 47 and count forward to 50. Color those numbers yellow.

Counting and Cardinality

Count to 50 by Ones

1	2	3	4	5	6	7	8	9	10
11	12	13	14	15	16	17	18	19	20
21	22	23	24	25	26	27	28	29	30
31	32	33	34	35	36	37	38	39	40
41	42	43	44	45	46	47	48	49	50

DIRECTIONS **I.** Look away and point to any number. Circle that number. Count forward from that number. Draw a line under the number 50.

2

Lesson 2

COMMON CORE STANDARD CC.K.CC.1

Lesson Objective: Know the count sequence when counting to 100 by ones.

Count to 100 by Ones

1	2	3	4	5	6	7	8	9	10
11	12	13	14	15	16	17	18	19	20
21	22	23	24	25	26	27	28	29	30
31	32	33	34	35	36	37	38	39	40
41	42	43	44	45	46	47	48	49	50
51	52	53	54	55	56	57	58	59	60
61	62	63	64	65	66	67	68	69	70
71	72	73	74	75	76	77	78	79	80
81	82	83	84	85	86	87	88	89	90
91	92	93	94	95	96	97	98	99	100

DIRECTIONS 1. Count forward from 1. Draw a dot on each number as you count. Begin with 97 and count forward to 100. Color those numbers yellow.

Counting and Cardinality

Name _____

Count to 100 by Ones

1	2	3	4	5	6	7	8	9	10
11	12	13	14	15	16	17	18	19	20
21	22	23	24	25	26	27	28	29	30
31	32	33	34	35	36	37	38	39	40
41	42	43	44	45	46	47	48	49	50
51	52	53	54	55	56	57	58	59	60
61	62	63	64	65	66	67	68	69	70
71	72	73	74	75	76	77	78	79	80
81	82	83	84	85	86	87	88	89	90
91	92	93	94	95	96	97	98	99	100

DIRECTIONS 1. Point to each number as you count to 100. Look away and point to any number. Circle that number. Count forward to 100 from that number. Draw a line under the number 100.

4

Lesson 3
COMMON CORE STANDARD CC.K.CC.1

Lesson Objective: Know the count sequence when counting to 100 by tens.

Count to 100 by Tens

1	2	3	4	5	6	7	8	9	10
11	12	13	14	15	16	17	18	19	20
21	22	23	24	25	26	27	28	29	30
31	32	33	34	35	36	37	38	39	40
41	42	43	44	45	46	47	48	49	50
51	52	53	54	55	56	57	58	59	60
61	62	63	64	65	66	67	68	69	70
71	72	73	74	75	76	77	78	79	80
81	82	83	84	85	86	87	88	89	90
91	92	93	94	95	96	97	98	99	100

DIRECTIONS 1. Color the boxes of all the numbers that end with a zero. Count by tens as you point to the numbers in the boxes you colored.

Counting and Cardinality

Count to 100 by Tens

51	52	53	54	55	56	57	58	59	60
61	62	63	64	65	66	67	68	69	70
71	72	73	74	75	76	77	78	79	80
81	82	83	84	85	86	87	88	89	90
91	92	93	94	95	96	97	98	99	100

DIRECTIONS 1. Trace the numbers to complete the counting order to 100. Count by tens as you point to the numbers you traced.

Count by Tens

1

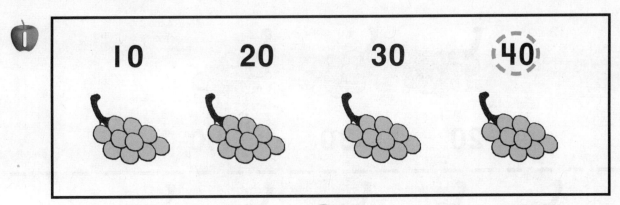

10   20   30   (40)

30   (40)   50

2

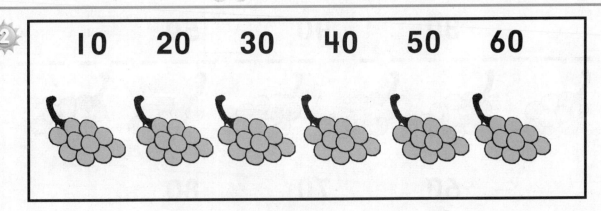

10   20   30   40   50   60

40   50   60

3

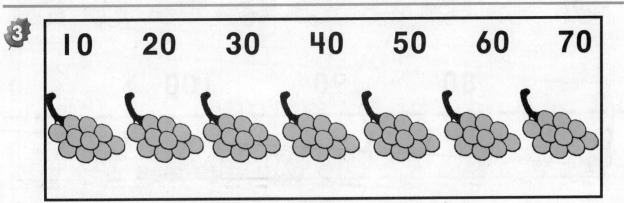

10   20   30   40   50   60   70

70   80   90

DIRECTIONS 1–3. Point to each number above the sets of 10 as you count by tens. Circle the last number you count. Circle the number below that shows how many.

Counting and Cardinality

7

Name ______________________________

Lesson 4
CC.K.CC.1

Count by Tens

1

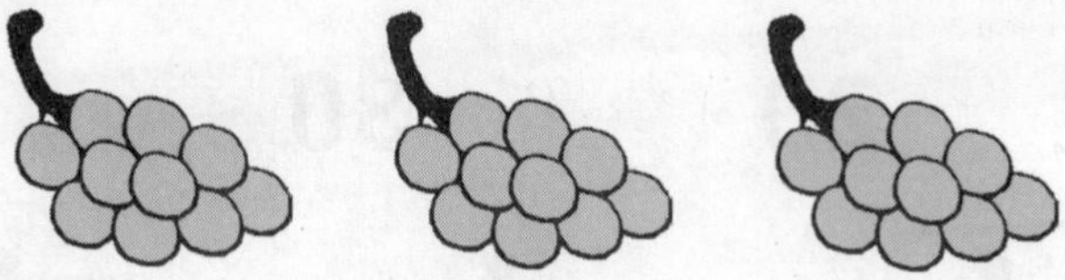

20 30 40

2

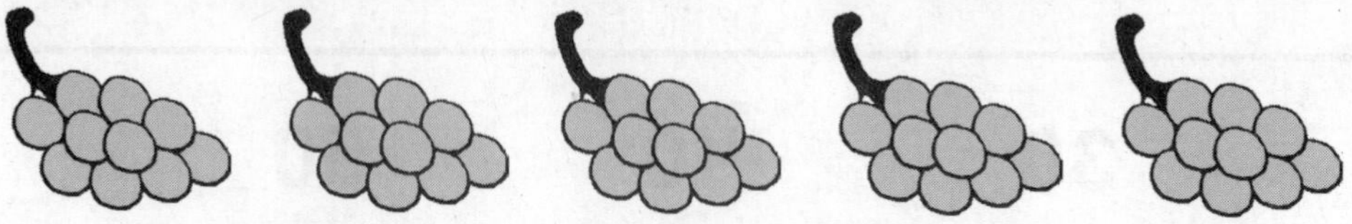

30 40 50

3

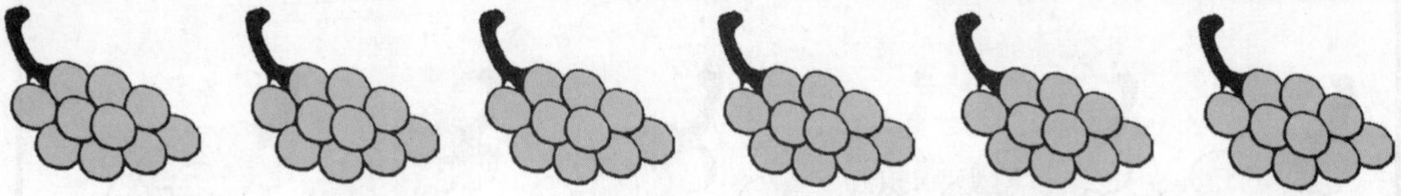

60 70 80

4

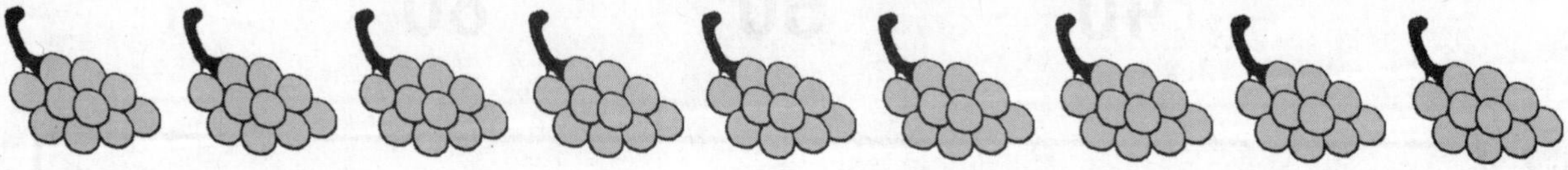

80 90 100

5

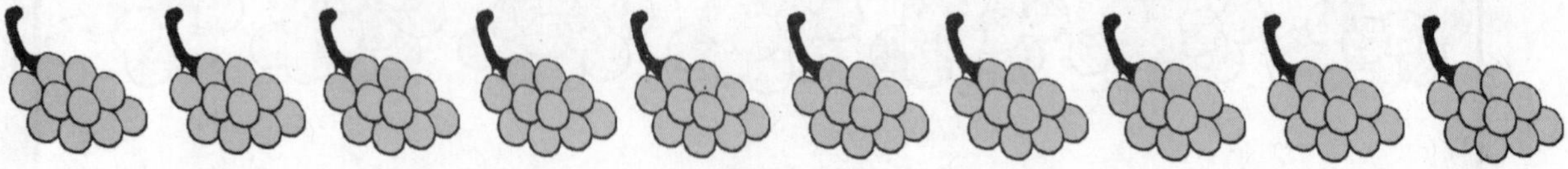

80 90 100

DIRECTIONS 1–5. Point to each set of 10 as you count by tens. Circle the number that shows how many.

Name _____

Lesson 5

COMMON CORE STANDARD CC.K.CC.2

Lesson Objective: Count forward to 10 from a given number.

Count and Order to 10

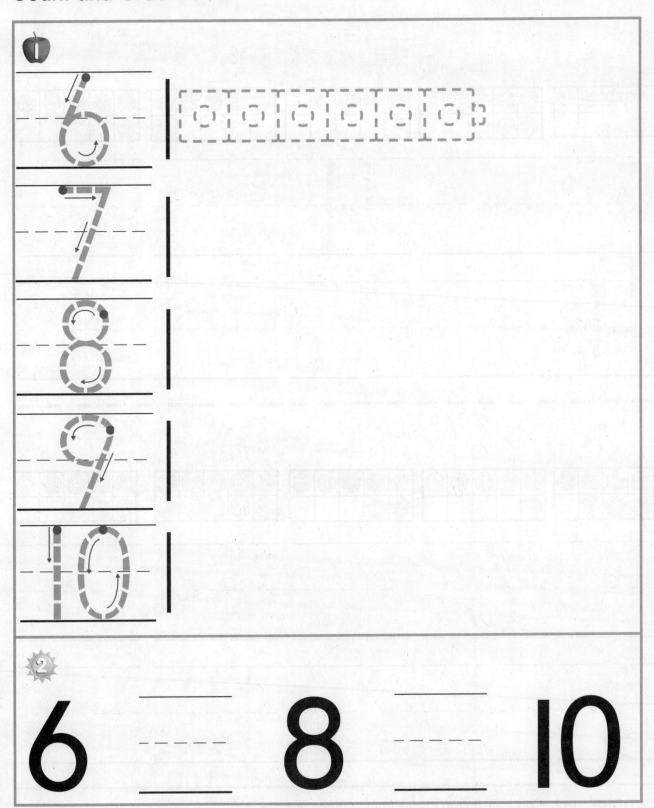

DIRECTIONS **1.** Trace the numbers. Make a cube train to show each number. Draw each cube train. **2.** Write the numbers in order as you count forward from 6.

Counting and Cardinality

Name _____

Count and Order to 10

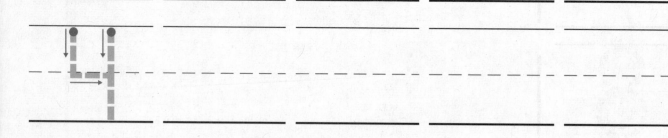

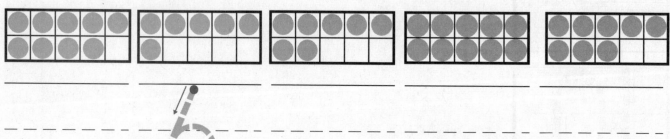

DIRECTIONS 1–2. Count the dots in the ten frames. Trace or write the numbers. Write the numbers in order as you count forward from the dashed number.

Lesson 6

COMMON CORE STANDARD CC.K.CC.2

Lesson Objective: Count forward to 20 from a given number.

Count and Order to 20

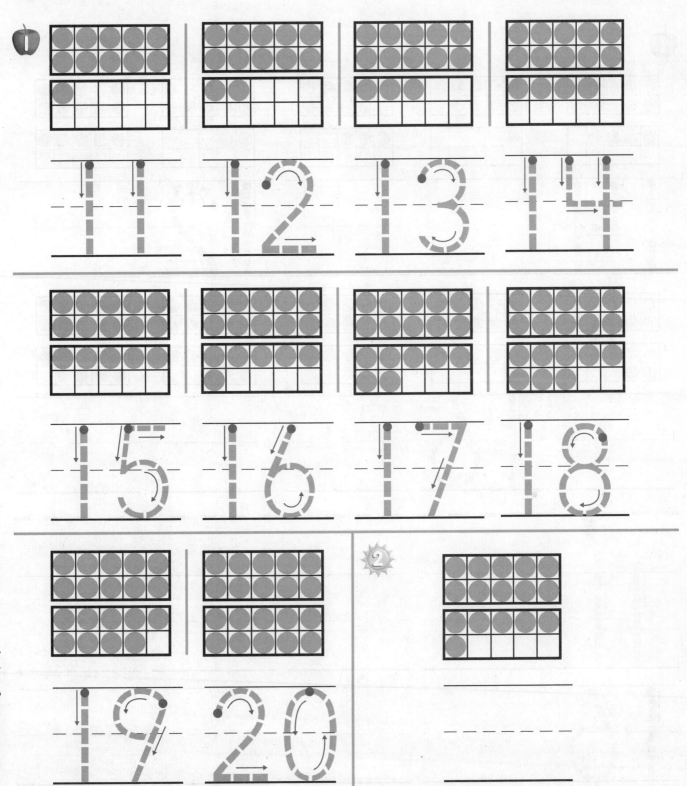

DIRECTIONS 1. Count the dots in each set of ten frames. Trace the numbers. Then point to each number as you count in order from 10. 2. Write the number that comes after 15.

Counting and Cardinality

Name _____

Count and Order to 20

1

2

DIRECTIONS   **1.** Count the dots in each set of ten frames. Trace or write the numbers.   **2.** Trace and write those numbers in order.

Lesson 7

COMMON CORE STANDARD CC.K.CC.3

Lesson Objective: Represent 1 and 2 objects with number names and written numerals.

Count and Write 1 and 2

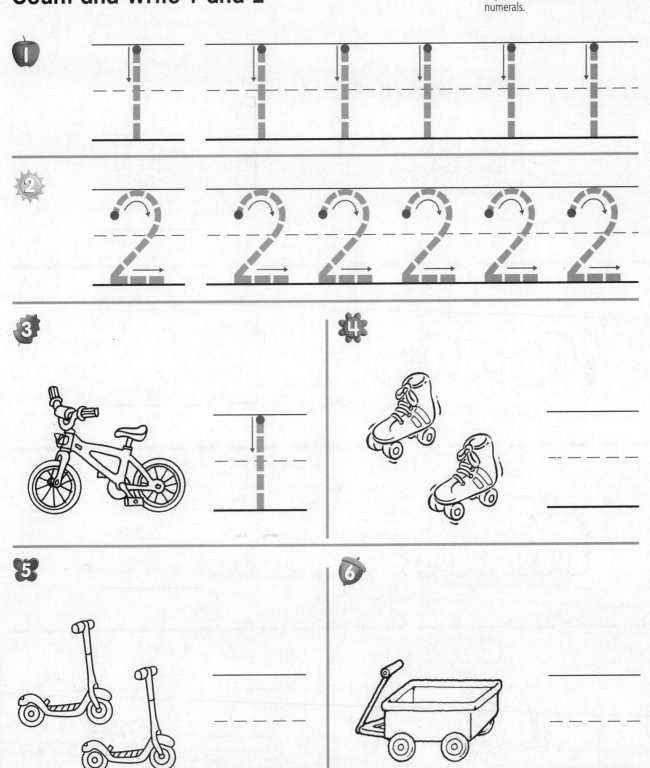

DIRECTIONS **1-2.** Say the number. Trace the numbers. **3.** Draw a dot on each object as you count. Tell how many. Trace the number. **4-6.** Draw a dot on each object as you count. Write the number.

Counting and Cardinality

Count and Write 1 and 2

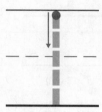

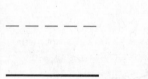

DIRECTIONS 1–4. Count and tell how many. Write the number.

Problem Solving • Understand 0

© Houghton Mifflin Harcourt Publishing Company

DIRECTIONS   **1.** Place a cube on the dinner table. Take the cube off the dinner table. How many cubes are on the dinner table now? Trace the number.   **2.** Place a cube on each plate. Take the cubes off the plates. How many cubes are on the plates now? Write the number.   **3.** Place a cube on each bowl. Take the cubes off the bowls. How many cubes are on the bowls now? Write the number.

Counting and Cardinality

Problem Solving • Understand 0

_____

- - - - - - -

_____

- -

2

_____

- - - - - - -

_____

DIRECTIONS Use counters to model these problems.   **I.** Oliver has one juice box. Lucy has one fewer juice box than Oliver. How many juice boxes does Lucy have? Write the number.   **2.** Jessica has no books. Wesley has 2 more books than Jessica. How many books does Wesley have? Write the number.

18

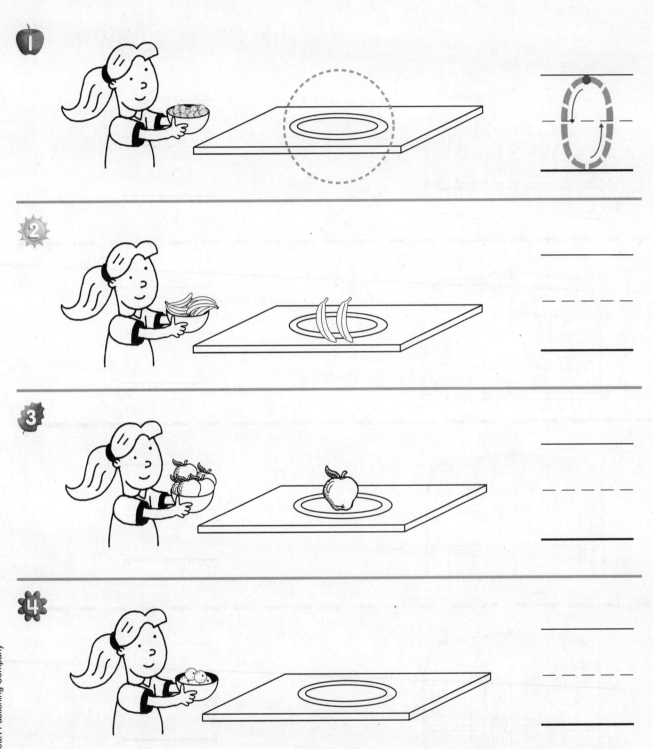

Lesson 10

COMMON CORE STANDARD CC.K.CC.3
Lesson Objective: Represent 0 objects
with a number name and a written numeral.

Identify and Write 0

DIRECTIONS **1.** Touch each piece of fruit on the plate. How many did you touch? Trace the number. Circle the plate if it has 0 pieces of fruit. **2–4.** Which plates have 0 pieces of fruit? Circle the plates. Write how many pieces of fruit.

Counting and Cardinality

Identify and Write 0

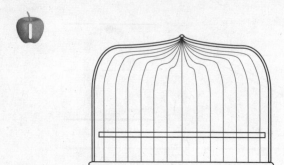

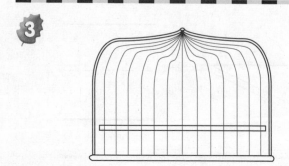

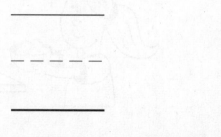

DIRECTIONS 1–4. How many birds are in the cage? Write the number. Circle the cages that have 0 birds.

Count and Write 6

1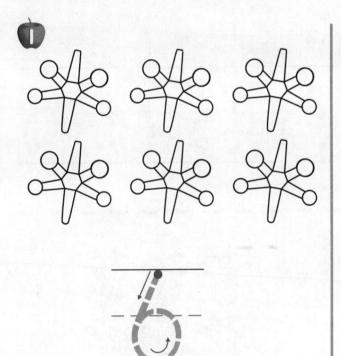

6

2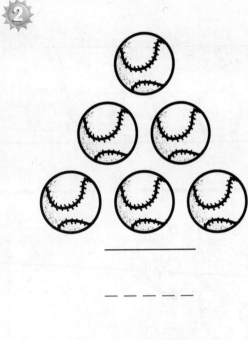

___ ___ ___

3

___ ___ ___

4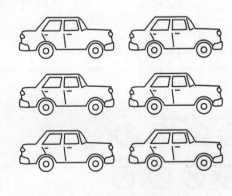

___ ___ ___

DIRECTIONS   1–4. Draw a dot on each toy as you count. Write the number.

Counting and Cardinality

Count and Write 6

1

6 six
6 6 6 6 6 6 6

2

_____

_ _ _ _ _ _ _

_____

3

_____

_ _ _ _ _ _ _

_____

4

_____

_ _ _ _ _ _ _

_____

5
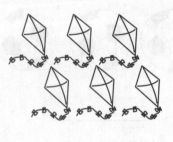

_____

_ _ _ _ _ _ _

_____

DIRECTIONS   1. Say the number. Trace the numbers.
2–5. Count and tell how many. Write the number.

Name _____

Count and Write 7

Lesson 12

COMMON CORE STANDARD CC.K.CC.3

Lesson Objective: Represent 7 objects with a number name and a written numeral.

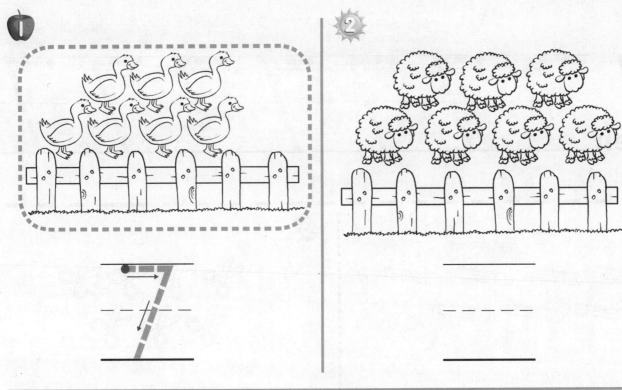

①

②

_____

- - - - - - - - - -

_____

③

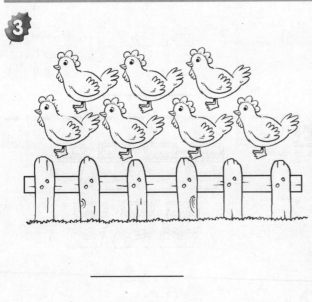

_____

- - - - - - - - - -

_____

④

_____

- - - - - - - - - -

_____

DIRECTIONS 1–4. Draw a dot on each animal as you count.
Write the number. Circle the sets of 7 animals.

Counting and Cardinality

23

Count and Write 7

7
seven

7 7 7 7 7 7 7

②

_____

- - - - - - - - - -

_____

③

_____

- - - - - - - - - -

_____

④

_____

- - - - - - - - - -

_____

⑤

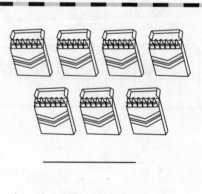

_____

- - - - - - - - - -

_____

DIRECTIONS I. Say the number. Trace the numbers.
2–5. Count and tell how many. Write the number.

Lesson 13

COMMON CORE STANDARD CC.K.CC.3

Lesson Objective: Represent 8 objects with a number name and a written numeral.

Name _____

Count and Write 8

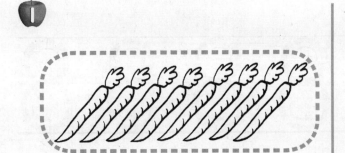

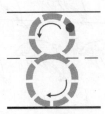

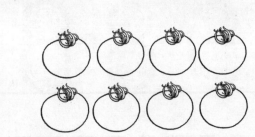

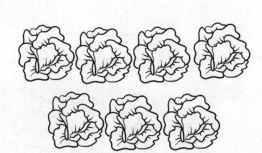

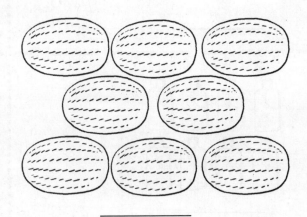

DIRECTIONS 1–4. Draw a dot on each object as you count.
Write the number. Circle the sets of 8 objects.

Counting and Cardinality

Count and Write 8

1

8
eight

8 8 8 8 8 8 8

2

_____

- - - - - - - -

_____

3

_____

- - - - - - - -

_____

4

_____

- - - - - - - -

_____

5

_____

- - - - - - - -

_____

DIRECTIONS I. Say the number. Trace the numbers.
2–5. Count and tell how many. Write the number.

Name _____

Lesson Objective: Represent 9 objects with a number name and a written numeral.

Count and Write 9

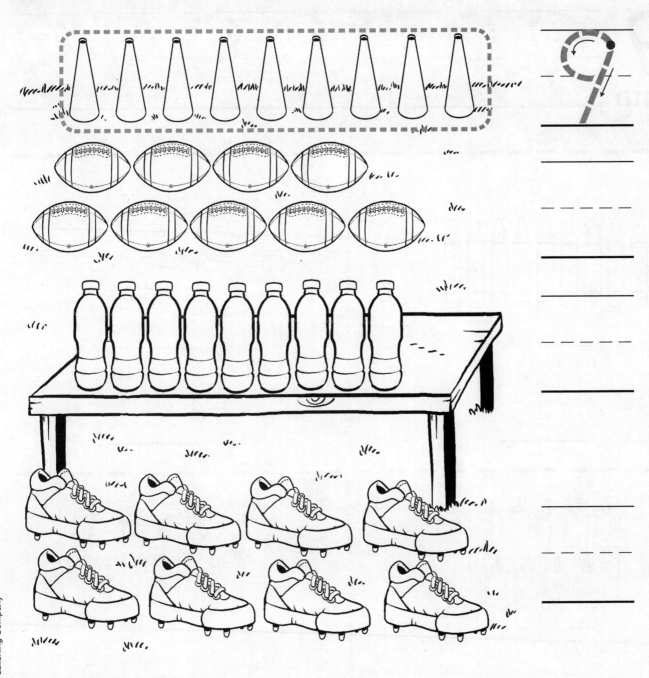

DIRECTIONS   1. Draw a dot on each object as you count.
Write the number. Circle the sets of 9 objects.

Counting and Cardinality

Count and Write 9

9 nine _____

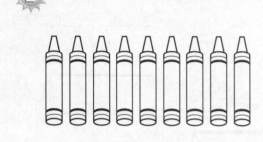

_____

- - - - - - - - - - -

_____

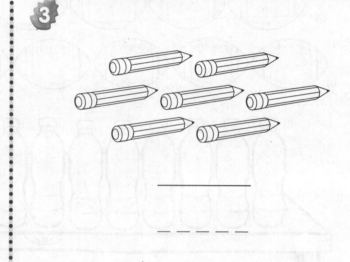

_____

- - - - - - - - - - -

_____

_____

- - - - - - - - - - -

_____

_____

- - - - - - - - - - -

_____

DIRECTIONS **1.** Say the number. Trace the numbers.
2–5. Count and tell how many. Write the number.

Count and Write 10

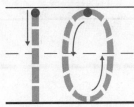

10
ten

_____

- - - - - - - - -

_____

_____

- - - - - - - - -

_____

DIRECTIONS **1.** Draw a dot on each acorn as you count. Tell how many. Trace the number. **2–5.** Draw a dot on each acorn as you count. Tell how many. Write the number.

Counting and Cardinality

Name _____

Count and Write 10

 1

10
ten

$10 \quad 10 \quad 10 \quad 10$

2

_____

- - - - - - - - - - -

_____

3

_____

- - - - - - - - - - -

_____

4

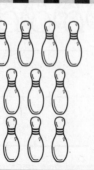

_____

- - - - - - - - - - -

_____

DIRECTIONS **1.** Say the number. Trace the numbers.
2–4. Count and tell how many. Write the number.

Count and Write 11 and 12

 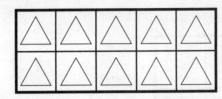 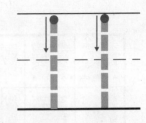

11
eleven

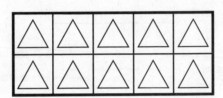 

DIRECTIONS **1.** Count and tell how many. Draw a dot on each object as you count. Trace the number. **2.** Look at the objects in the ten frame in Exercise 1. Count and write the number. **3.** Look at the object below the ten frame in Exercise 1. Count and write the number. **4.** Look at the ten ones and some more ones in Exercise 1. Complete the addition sentence to match.

Counting and Cardinality

Count and Write 11 and 12

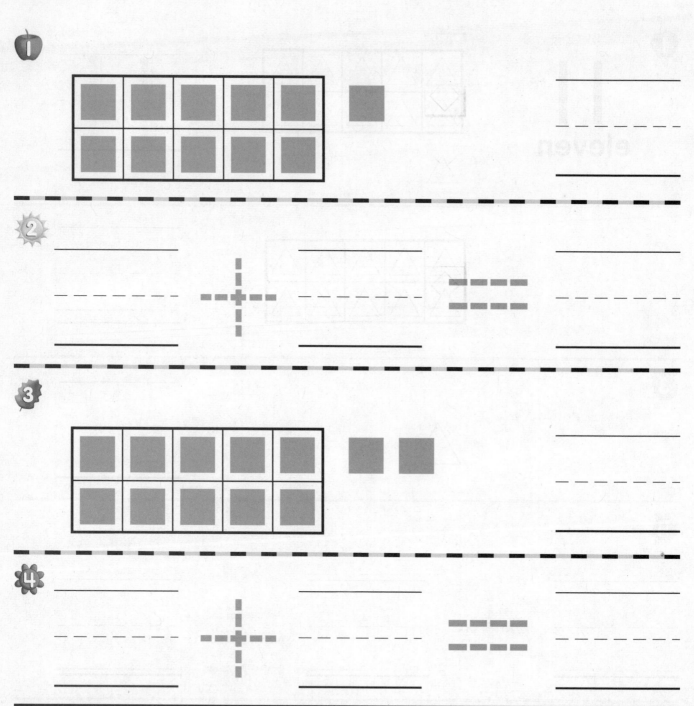

DIRECTIONS 1. Count and tell how many. Write the number.
2. Look at the ten ones and some more ones in Exercise 1.
Complete the addition sentence to match. 3. Count and tell how
many. Write the number. 4. Look at the ten ones and some more
ones in Exercise 3. Complete the addition sentence to match.

Name _____

Lesson 17

COMMON CORE STANDARD CC.K.CC.3

Lesson Objective: Represent 13 and 14 objects with number names and written numerals.

Count and Write 13 and 14

 1

13
thirteen

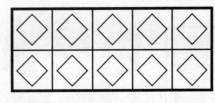

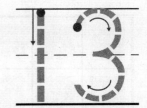

 2

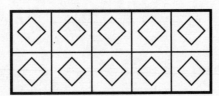

_____

- - - - - - - - - - - - -

_____

3

_____

- - - - - - - - - - - - -

_____

 4

DIRECTIONS **1.** Count and tell how many. Draw a dot on each object as you count. Trace the number. **2.** Look at the objects in the ten frame in Exercise 1. Count and write the number. **3.** Look at the objects below the ten frame in Exercise 1. Count and write the number. **4.** Look at the ten ones and some more ones in Exercise 1. Complete the addition sentence to match.

Counting and Cardinality

Count and Write 13 and 14

 1

_____

_____

- -

 2

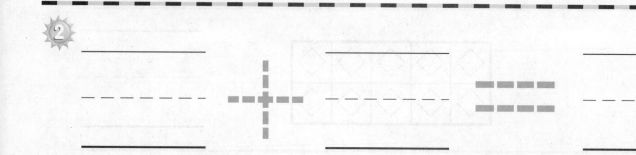

- -

3

- -

4

DIRECTIONS **1.** Count and tell how many. Write the number.
2. Look at the ten ones and some more ones in Exercise 1.
Complete the addition sentence to match.   **3.** Count and tell how
many. Write the number.   **4.** Look at the ten ones and some more
ones in Exercise 3. Complete the addition sentence to match.

Problem Solving • Use Numbers to 15

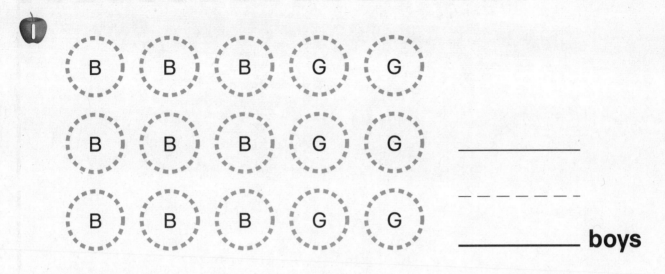

_____

- - - - - - - - -

_____ **boys**

_____

- - - - - - - - -

_____ **girls**

DIRECTIONS **1.** There are 15 children in Mrs. Joiner's class. They sit in rows of 5. There are 3 boys and 2 girls in each row. How many boys are in the class? Trace the 3 rows of 5 circles. *B* is for boy and *G* is for girl. Count the boys. Write the number. **2.** There are 15 children in Mr. Gilbert's class. They sit in rows of 5. There are 4 boys and 1 girl in each row. How many girls are in the class? Draw to solve the problem.

Counting and Cardinality

Name ______________________________

Lesson 18
CC.K.CC.3

Problem Solving • Use Numbers to 15

______ carrot plants

DIRECTIONS There are 15 vegetables in the garden. They are planted in rows of 5. There are 2 carrot plants and 3 potato plants in each row. How many carrot plants are in the garden? Draw to solve the problem.

Lesson 19

COMMON CORE STANDARD CC.K.CC.3

Lesson Objective: Represent 16 and 17 objects with number names and written numerals.

Count and Write 16 and 17

16
sixteen

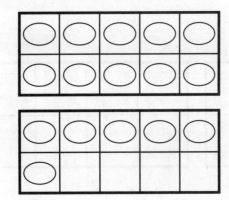

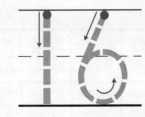

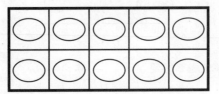

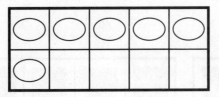

DIRECTIONS 1. Count and tell how many. Draw a dot on each object as you count. Trace the number. 2. Look at the objects in the top ten frame in Exercise 1. Count and write the number. 3. Look at the objects in the bottom ten frame in Exercise 1. Count and write the number. 4. Look at the ten frames in Exercise 1. Complete the addition sentence to match.

Counting and Cardinality

Name _____

Count and Write 16 and 17

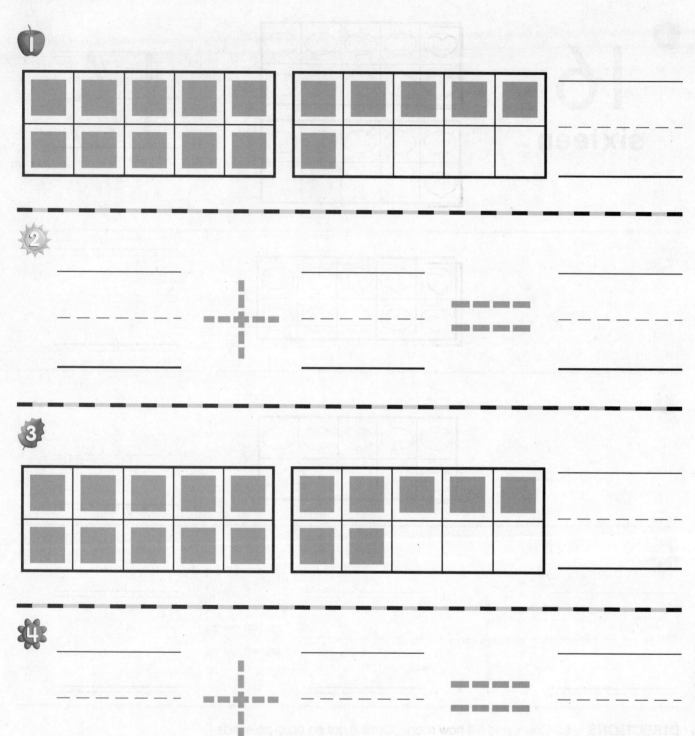

1

2

3

4

DIRECTIONS **1.** Count and tell how many. Write the number. **2.** Look at the ten frames in Exercise 1. Complete the addition sentence to match. **3.** Count and tell how many. Write the number. **4.** Look at the ten frames in Exercise 3. Complete the addition sentence to match.

38

Count and Write 18 and 19

 1

18
eighteen

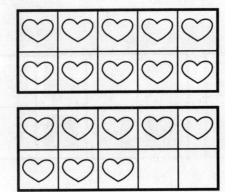

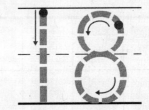

 2

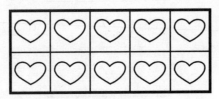

 3

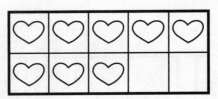

4

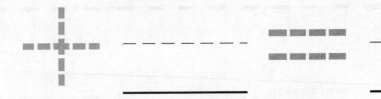

DIRECTIONS **1.** Count and tell how many. Draw a dot on each object as you count. Trace the number. **2.** Look at the objects in the top ten frame in Exercise 1. Count and write the number. **3.** Look at the objects in the bottom ten frame in Exercise 1. Count and write the number. **4.** Look at the ten frames in Exercise 1. Complete the addition sentence to match.

Counting and Cardinality

Count and Write 18 and 19

1.

_____ _____

_____

2.

_____ _____ _____ _____

_____ + _____ = _____

3.

_____ _____

_____

4.

_____ _____ _____ _____

_____ + _____ = _____

DIRECTIONS 1. Count and tell how many. Write the number.   **2.** Look at the ten frames in Exercise 1. Complete the addition sentence to match.   **3.** Count and tell how many. Write the number.   **4.** Look at the ten frames in Exercise 3. Complete the addition sentence to match.

Name _____

Lesson 21

COMMON CORE STANDARD CC.K.CC.3

Lesson Objective: Represent 20 objects with a number name and a written numeral.

Count and Write 20

1

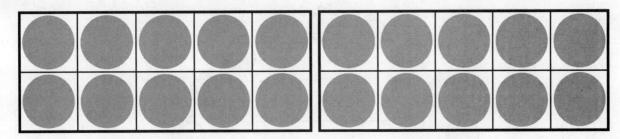

20
twenty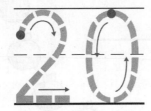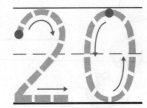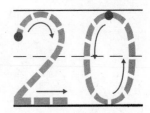

2

 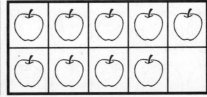   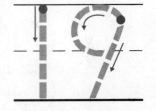

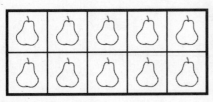 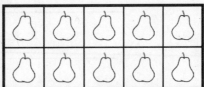   

DIRECTIONS **1.** Count and tell how many counters. Draw a dot on each counter as you count them. Trace the numbers as you say them.   **2–3.** Count and tell how many pieces of fruit. Touch each fruit as you count. Trace the number.

Counting and Cardinality

41

© Houghton Mifflin Harcourt Publishing Company

Count and Write 20

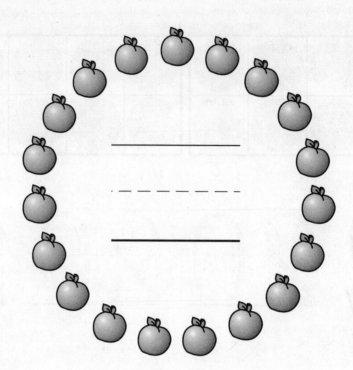

_____

– – – – – – – –

_____

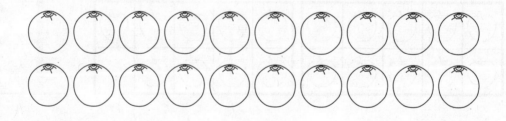

_____

– – – – – – – –

_____

DIRECTIONS 1–2. Count and tell how many pieces of fruit. Write the number.

Lesson 22

COMMON CORE STANDARD CC.K.CC.4a
Lesson Objective: Model and count 1 and 2 with objects.

Name _____

Model and Count 1 and 2

 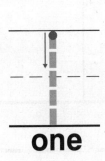

one

two

one

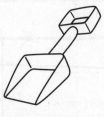

DIRECTIONS Draw a dot on each toy as you count. Use cubes to show the number of objects. **1.** Say the number. Trace the number and the cube. **2–3.** Say the number. Trace the number. Draw the cubes.

Counting and Cardinality

Model and Count 1 and 2

1 2 two

2 1 one

3 2 two

4 1 one

DIRECTIONS 1-4. Say the number. Count out that many counters in the five frame. Draw the counters.

Model and Count 3 and 4

three

 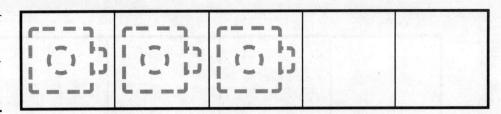

three

  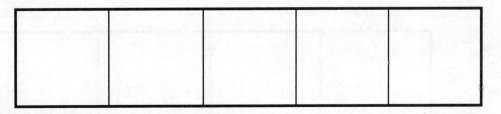

four

 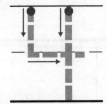 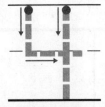

four

DIRECTIONS   I. Say the number as you trace it. Count out that many cubes in the five frame. Trace the cubes.   **2–4.** Say the number as you trace it. Count that many cubes in the five frame. Draw the cubes.

Counting and Cardinality

Name ______________________________

Model and Count 3 and 4

1

3

three

2

4

four

3

3

three

4

4

four

DIRECTIONS 1–4. Say the number as you trace it. Count out that many counters in the five frame. Draw the counters.

Model and Count 5

1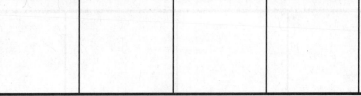

five

2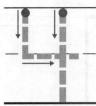

four

3

three

4

five

DIRECTIONS **1.** Say the number as you trace it. Place cubes to show the number. Trace the cubes. **2–4.** Say the number as you trace it. Place cubes to show the number. Draw the cubes.

Counting and Cardinality

Model and Count 5

1

_____

- - - - - - - -

_____

2

_____

- - - - - - - -

_____

3

_____

- - - - - - - -

_____

4

_____

- - - - - - - -

_____

DIRECTIONS **I.** Place counters to show five. Draw the counters. Write the number. **2.** Place counters to show three. Draw the counters. Write the number. **3.** Place counters to show four. Draw the counters. Write the number. **4.** Place counters to show five. Draw the counters. Write the number.

Lesson 25

COMMON CORE STANDARD CC.K.CC.4b
Lesson Objective: Represent 5 objects with
a number name and a written numeral.

Count and Write 5

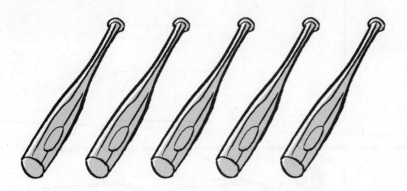

five

DIRECTIONS **1.** Draw a dot on each baseball bat as you count. Tell how many. Trace the number. Draw one baseball above each bat to show a set of 5 baseballs. **2.** Circle the sets of 5 objects.

Counting and Cardinality

49

Name _____

Count and Write 5

1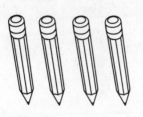

_____

– – – – – –

_____

2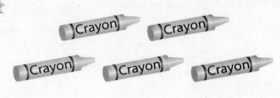

_____

– – – – – –

_____

3

_____

– – – – – –

_____

4

_____

– – – – – –

_____

5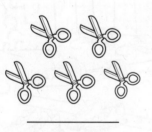

_____

– – – – – –

_____

6

_____

– – – – – –

_____

DIRECTIONS 1–6. Count and tell how many. Write the number.

Name _____

Count and Order to 5

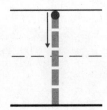   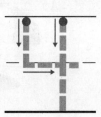 

  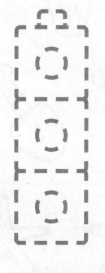 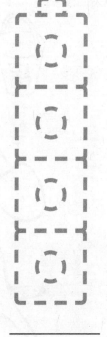 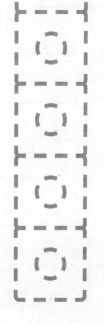

DIRECTIONS **1.** Trace the numbers. Make a cube tower to show each number. **2.** Place the cube towers in order. Trace the cube towers. Write the number of cubes for each tower.

Counting and Cardinality

Name _____

Count and Order to 5

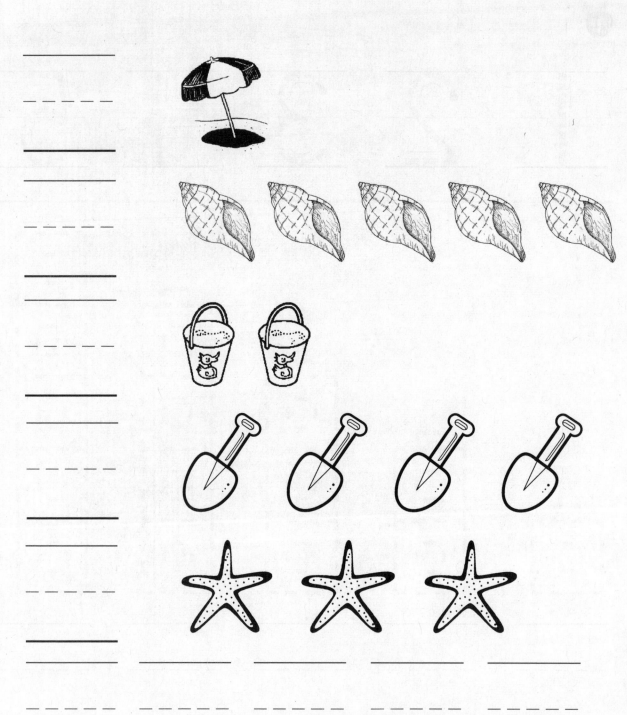

DIRECTIONS   I.   Count the objects in each set. Write the number beside the set of objects. Write those numbers in order beginning with number 1.

© Houghton Mifflin Harcourt Publishing Company

Name _____

Model and Count 6

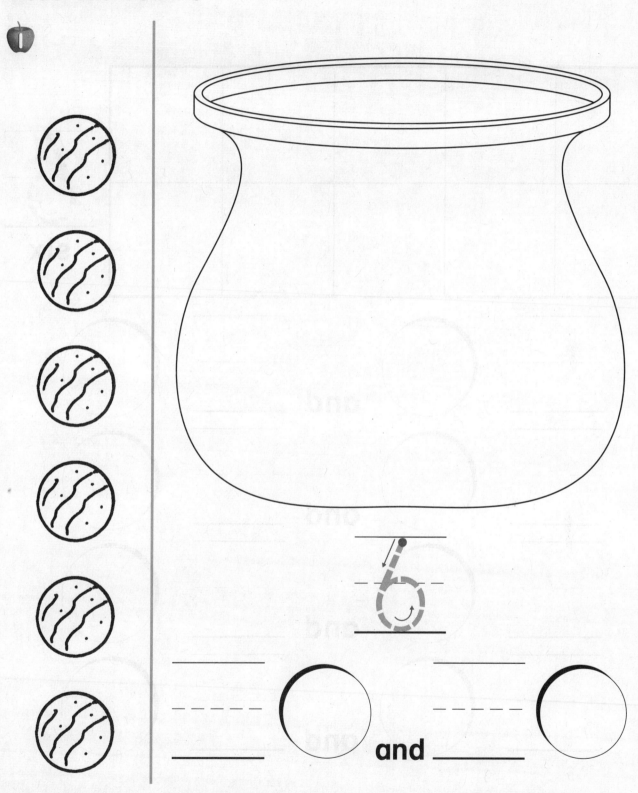

and _____

DIRECTIONS I. Place a red counter on each marble. Move the counters to the basket. Trace the number. Turn some of the counters over. Color to show the counters below. Write to show a pair of numbers that makes 6.

Counting and Cardinality

Model and Count 6

six

and

and

and

and

DIRECTIONS   I. Trace the number 6. Use two-color counters to model the different ways to make 6. Color to show the counters below. Write to show some pairs of numbers that make 6.

Name _____

COMMON CORE STANDARD CC.K.CC.5
Lesson Objective: Model and count 7 with objects.

Model and Count 7

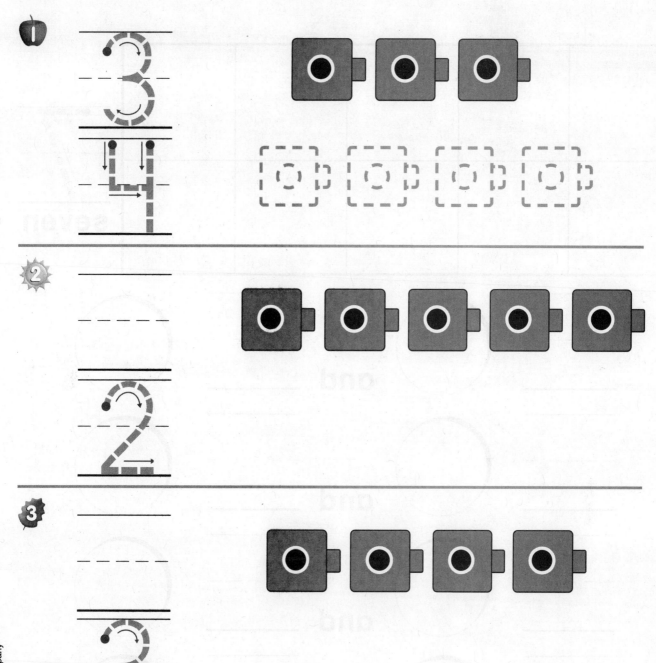

DIRECTIONS **1.** Draw a dot on each cube as you count. Trace the number. Place more cubes below to make 7. Trace the cubes. Trace the number.
2–3. Draw a dot on each cube as you count. Write the number. Place more cubes below to make 7. Draw the cubes. Trace the number.

Counting and Cardinality

55

Name _____

Model and Count 7

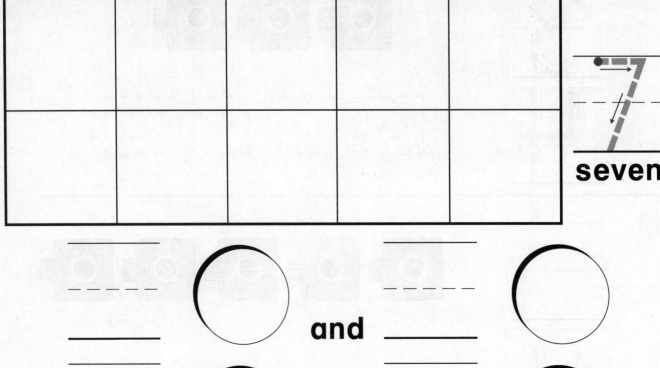

seven

_____   _____
and
_____   _____

_____   _____
and
_____   _____

_____   _____
and
_____   _____

_____   _____
and
_____   _____

DIRECTIONS   1. Trace the number 7. Use two-color counters
to model the different ways to make 7. Color to show the counters
below. Write to show some pairs of numbers that make 7.

56

Model and Count 8

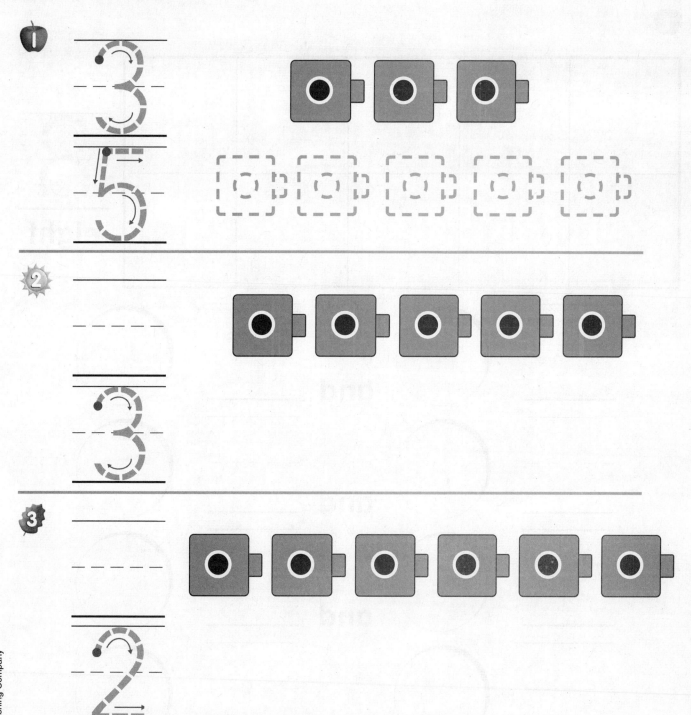

© Houghton Mifflin Harcourt Publishing Company

DIRECTIONS **1.** Draw a dot on each cube as you count. Trace the number. Place more cubes below to make 8. Trace the cubes. Trace the number.
2–3. Draw a dot on each cube as you count. Write the number. Place more cubes below to make 8. Draw the cubes. Trace the number.

Counting and Cardinality

Model and Count 8

8
eight

___ ___ ___ ___

___ ___ ◯ **and** ___ ___ ◯

___ ___ ◯ **and** ___ ___ ◯

___ ___ ◯ **and** ___ ___ ◯

___ ___ ◯ **and** ___ ___ ◯

DIRECTIONS   **I.** Trace the number 8. Use two-color counters to model the different ways to make 8. Color to show the counters below. Write to show some pairs of numbers that make 8.

Model and Count 9

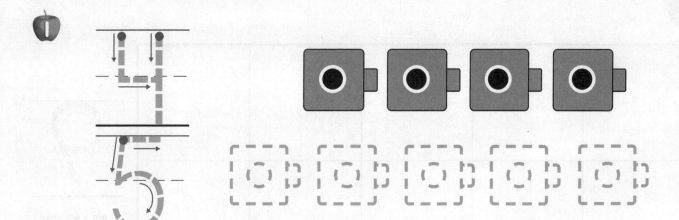

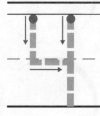

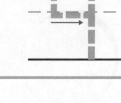

DIRECTIONS **1.** Draw a dot on each cube as you count. Trace the number. Place more cubes below to make 9. Trace the cubes. Trace the number. **2–3.** Draw a dot on each cube as you count. Write the number. Place more cubes below to make 9. Draw the cubes. Trace the number.

Model and Count 9

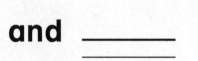

nine

____  **and** ____

____ ○ **and** ____ ○

____ ○ **and** ____ ○

____ ○ **and** ____ ○

DIRECTIONS 1. Trace the number 9. Use two-color counters to model the different ways to make 9. Color to show the counters below. Write to show some pairs of numbers that make 9.

60

Name _____

Model and Count 10

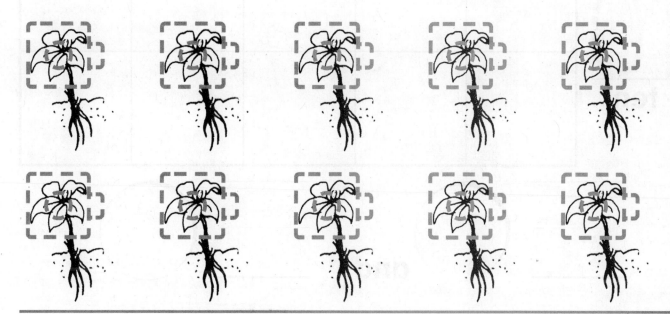

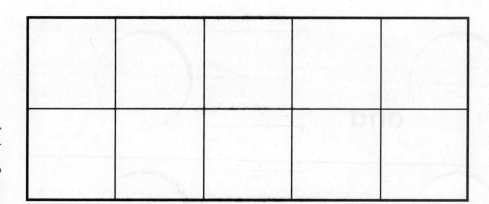

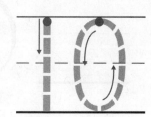

DIRECTIONS **I.** Place a cube on each plant. Trace the cubes. **2.** Move the cubes to the ten frame. Draw the cubes. Point to each cube as you count. Trace the number.

Counting and Cardinality

61

Name ___________________________

Lesson 31
CC.K.CC.5

Model and Count 10

10
ten

___ and ___

___ and ___

___ and ___

___ and ___

DIRECTIONS Trace the number. Use counters to model the different ways to make 10. Color to show the counters below. Write to show some pairs of numbers that make 10.

Lesson 33

COMMON CORE STANDARD CC.K.CC.6

Lesson Objective: Use matching and counting strategies to compare sets with the same number of objects.

Same Number

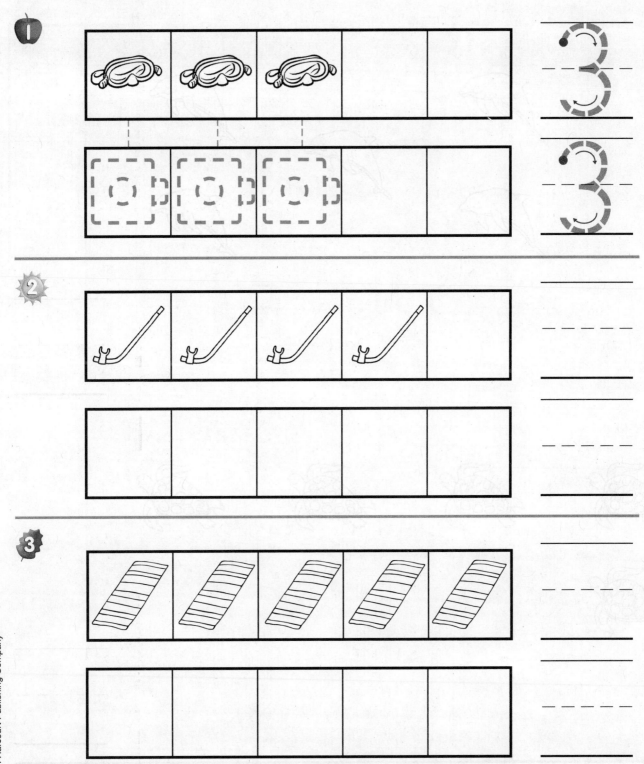

DIRECTIONS 1–3. Place a cube below each object to show the same number of objects. Trace or draw those cubes. Trace or draw a line to match an object to a cube in each set. Count and tell how many in each set. Trace or write the numbers.

Counting and Cardinality

Same Number

_____
- - - - - - - - - -
_____

_____
- - - - - - - - - -
_____

DIRECTIONS **1.** Compare the sets of objects. Is the number of dolphins greater than, less than, or the same as the number of turtles? Count how many dolphins. Write the number. Count how many turtles. Write the number. Tell a friend what you know about the number of objects in each set.

Lesson 34

COMMON CORE STANDARD CC.K.CC.6

Lesson Objective: Use matching and counting strategies to compare sets when the number of objects in one set is greater than the number of objects in the other set.

Greater Than

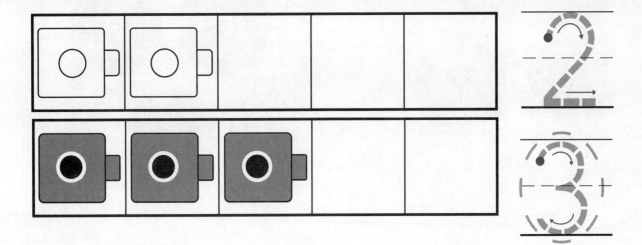

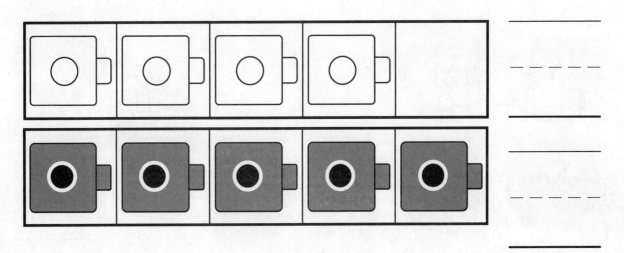

DIRECTIONS **1.** Place cubes as shown. Count and tell how many in each set. Trace the numbers. Trace the circle to show the number that is greater. **2.** Place cubes as shown. Count and tell how many in each set. Write the numbers. Circle the number that is greater.

© Houghton Mifflin Harcourt Publishing Company

Counting and Cardinality

Greater Than

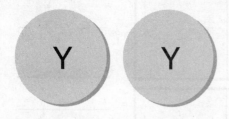

_____

_ _ _ _ _

_____

_____

_ _ _ _ _

_____

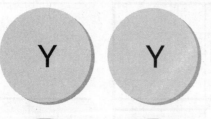

_____

_ _ _ _ _

_____

_____

_ _ _ _ _

_____

DIRECTIONS   1–2. Place counters as shown. Y is for yellow, and R is for red. Count and tell how many are in each set. Write the numbers. Compare the numbers. Circle the number that is greater.

Less Than

Lesson 35

COMMON CORE STANDARD CC.K.CC.6

Lesson Objective: Use matching and counting strategies to compare sets when the number of objects in one set is less than the number of objects in the other set.

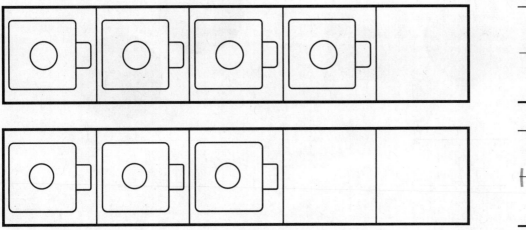

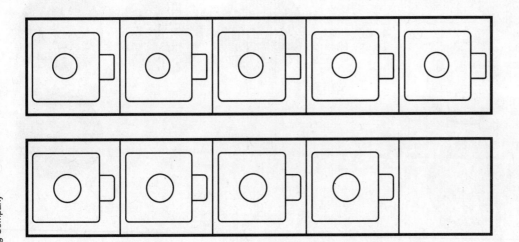

DIRECTIONS **1–2.** Place cubes on the five frames as shown. Count and tell how many in each set. Write the numbers. Compare the sets by matching. Circle the number that is less.

Name _____

Less Than

1

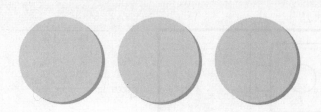

_____   _____

_ _ _ _ _   _ _ _ _ _

_____   _____

· ·

2

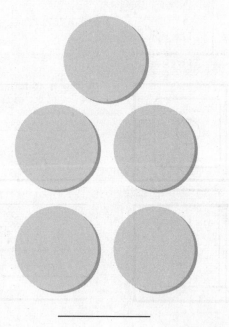

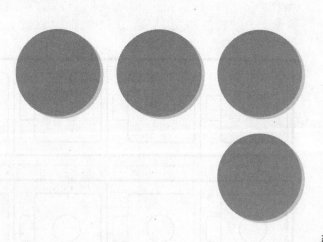

_____   _____

_ _ _ _ _   _ _ _ _ _

_____   _____

DIRECTIONS   1–2. Count and tell how many are in each set. Write
the numbers. Compare the numbers. Circle the number that is less.

70

Name _____

Problem Solving •
Compare by Matching Sets to 5

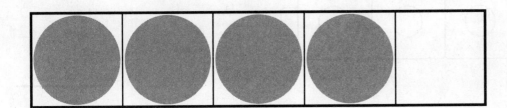

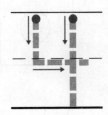

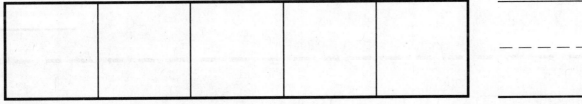

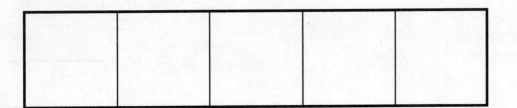

DIRECTIONS   **1.** How many counters are there? Trace the number.
2. Place counters to model a set that has a number of counters greater than 4.
Draw the counters. Write how many.   **3.** Place counters to model a set that
has a number of counters less than 4. Draw the counters. Write how many.

Counting and Cardinality

Problem Solving • Compare by Matching Sets to 5

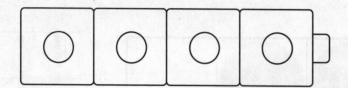

_____

- - - - - - - - -

_____

_____

- - - - - - - - -

_____

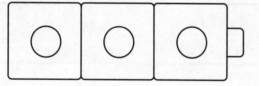

_____

- - - - - - - - -

_____

_____

- - - - - - - - -

_____

DIRECTIONS **1.** How many cubes are there? Write the number. Model a cube train that has a number of cubes greater than 4. Draw the cube train. Write how many. Compare the cube trains by matching. Tell a friend about the cube trains. **2.** How many cubes are there? Write the number. Model a cube train that has a number of cubes less than 3. Draw the cube train. Write how many. Compare the cube trains by matching. Tell a friend about the cube trains.

Name _____

Compare by Counting
Sets to 5

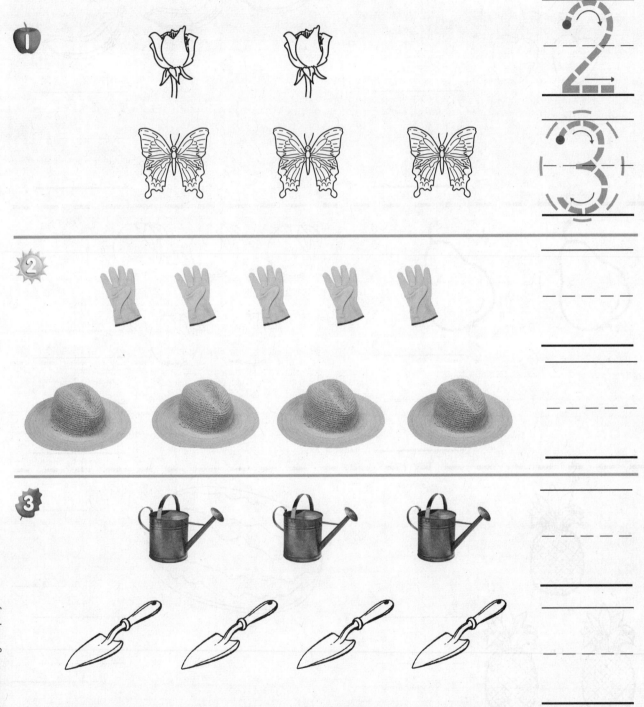

DIRECTIONS   1–2. Draw a dot on each object in the sets as you count. Trace or write the numbers. Compare the numbers. Circle the number that is greater.   3. Draw a dot on each object in the sets as you count. Write the numbers. Compare the numbers. Circle the number that is less.

Counting and Cardinality

73

Name _____

Compare by Counting Sets to 5

 1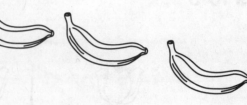

_ _ _ _ _ _ _ _ _ _

_____

_ _ _ _ _ _ _ _ _ _

_____

 2

_ _ _ _ _ _ _ _ _ _

_____

_ _ _ _ _ _ _ _ _ _

_____

 3

_____

_ _ _ _ _ _ _ _ _ _

_____

DIRECTIONS 1–2. Count how many objects are in each set. Write the numbers. Compare the numbers. Circle the number that is greater. **3.** Count how many objects are in each set. Write the numbers. Compare the numbers. Circle the number that is less.

Name _____

COMMON CORE STANDARD CC.K.CC.6
Lesson Objective: Use counting strategies to compare sets of objects.

Compare by Counting Sets to 10

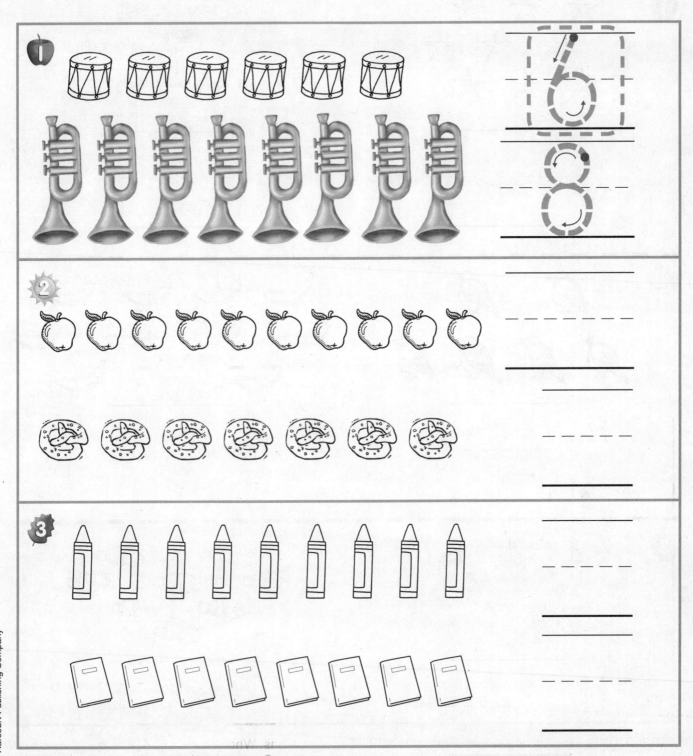

DIRECTIONS 1–2. Draw a dot on each object in the first set as you count. Trace or write the number. Draw a dot on each object in the second set as you count. Trace or write the number. Circle the number that is less. 3. Draw a dot on each object in the first set as you count. Write the number. Draw a dot on each object in the second set as you count. Write the number. Circle the greater number.

Counting and Cardinality

Name _____

Compare by Counting Sets to 10

 1

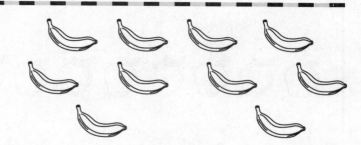

_____   _____

- - - - - - - - - - -   - - - - - - - - - - -

_____   _____

 2

_____   _____

- - - - - - - - - - -   - - - - - - - - - - -

_____   _____

 3

   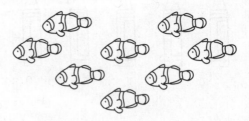

_____   _____

- - - - - - - - - - -   - - - - - - - - - - -

_____   _____

DIRECTIONS Count how many in each set. Write the number of
objects in each set. Compare the numbers. **1–2.** Circle the number
that is less. **3.** Circle the number that is greater.

Name _____

Problem Solving •
Compare Numbers to 20

COMMON CORE STANDARD CC.K.CC.6
Lesson Objective: Solve problems by using the strategy *make a model*.

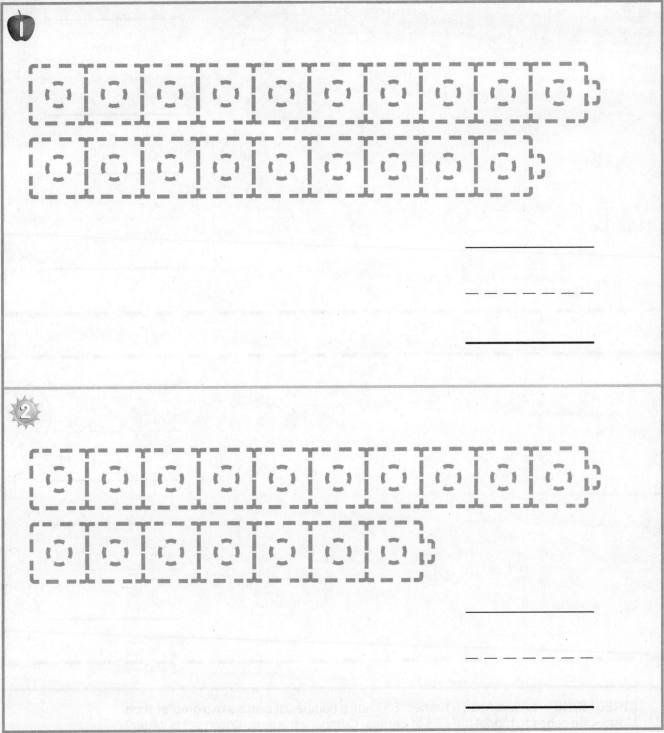

DIRECTIONS Use cubes to model the sets. **1.** Dana has 19 cubes. Trace the cubes. Write the number. **2.** Dana has a number of cubes two greater than Ethan. Trace the cubes. Write the number. Compare the sets of cubes in Exercises 1 and 2. Circle the greater number.

Counting and Cardinality

81

Problem Solving • Compare
Numbers to 20

DIRECTIONS 1. Teni has 16 berries. She has a number of berries two greater than Marta. Use cubes to model the sets of berries. Compare the sets. Which set is larger? Draw the cubes. Write how many in each set. Circle the greater number. Tell a friend how you compared the numbers. **2.** Ben has 18 pears. Sophia has a number of pears two less than Ben. Use cubes to model the sets of pears. Compare the sets. Which set is smaller? Draw the cubes. Write how many in each set. Circle the number that is less. Tell a friend how you compared the numbers.

Name _____

Compare Two Numbers

1 5   7

2 8   4

3 3   6

DIRECTIONS **1–2.** Look at the numbers. Trace or draw counters to model the numbers. Compare the sets. Draw a circle around the number that is less. **3.** Look at the numbers. Draw counters to model the numbers. Compare the sets. Draw a circle around the number that is greater.

Counting and Cardinality

83

Compare Two Numbers

 1

8   5

 2

10   7

 3

6   9

 4

4   6

 5

8   7

6

5   3

DIRECTIONS 1–3. Look at the numbers. Think about the counting order as you compare the numbers. Circle the greater number. 4–6. Look at the numbers. Think about the counting order as you compare the numbers. Circle the number that is less.

Addition: Add To

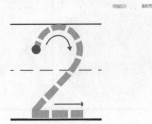

and

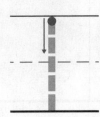

DIRECTIONS 1. Joy has a cup with two white counters. Then she adds one gray counter. Trace the number that shows how many white counters Joy has. Trace the number that shows the counter being added. **2.** Trace the counters in Joy's cup now. **3.** Write how many counters are in Joy's cup now.

Operations and Algebraic Thinking

Addition: Add To

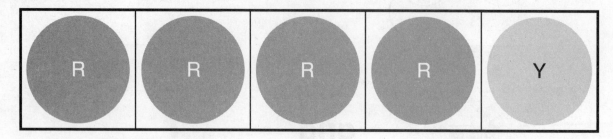

_____   _____

- - - - - - -   **and**   - - - - - - -

_____   _____

- -

_____

- - - - - - -

_____

DIRECTIONS   I. There are four red counters in the five frame. One yellow counter is added. R is for red, and Y is for yellow. How many of each color counter? Write the numbers.   **2.** Write the number that shows how many counters are in the five frame now.

Addition: Put Together

 1

 and

 2

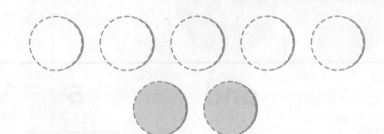

 3

DIRECTIONS   1–3. Kim has 5 white counters and 2 gray counters. How many counters does she have in all?   **1.** Count the white counters. Trace the number. Count the gray counters. Trace the number.   **2.** Trace the counters to model the sets that are put together. Write the numbers and trace the symbol.   **3.** Write how many counters Kim has in all.

Operations and Algebraic Thinking

87

Addition: Put Together

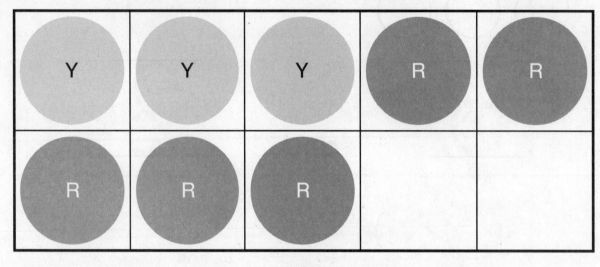

3   and   5

DIRECTIONS   Roy has three yellow counters and five red counters. How many counters does he have in all? **I.** Place counters in the ten frame to model the sets that are put together. Y is for yellow, and R is for red. Write the numbers and trace the symbol. Write the number to show how many in all.

Name _____

Problem Solving • Act Out Addition Problems

$$2 + 2$$

DIRECTIONS Act out the addition word problem. **1.** There were two books on the table. A girl brings two more books. How many books are on the table now? Trace the numbers and the symbol. **2.** Place a cube on each book on the table in Exercise 1. Write the number. Place a cube on each book the girl has. Write the number. Count how many cubes. Write the number to show how many books there are in all. Trace the symbols.

Operations and Algebraic Thinking

Problem Solving • Act Out
Addition Problems

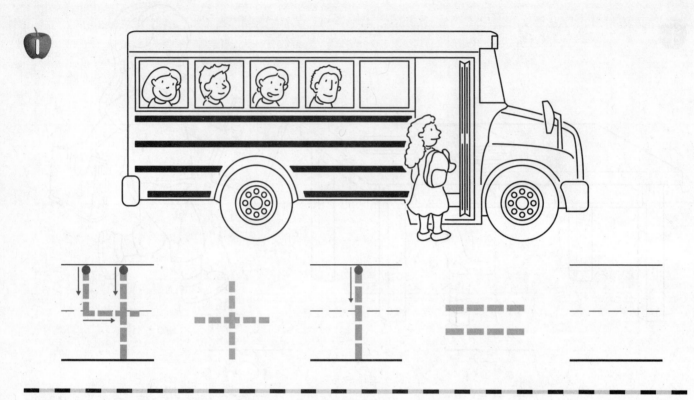

4 + 1 = ___

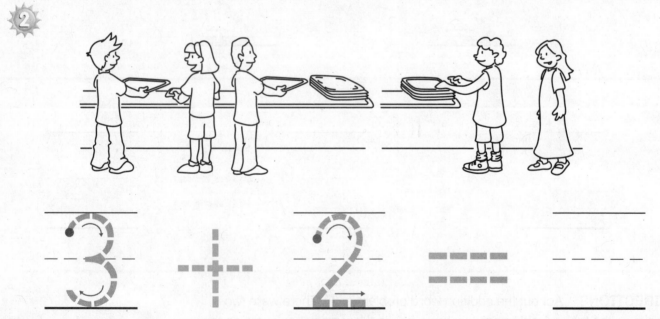

3 + 2 = ___

DIRECTIONS 1–2. Tell an addition word problem about the children. Trace the numbers and the symbols. Write the number that shows how many children in all.

© Houghton Mifflin Harcourt Publishing Company

Name _____

Subtraction: Take From

 take away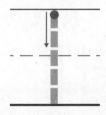

© Houghton Mifflin Harcourt Publishing Company

DIRECTIONS 1. Look at the picture. How many children in all? Draw a dot on each child as you count. Trace the 3. How many children are leaving? Circle the child who is leaving. Trace the 1. How many children are left? Draw a line under the two children sitting. Trace the 2.

Operations and Algebraic Thinking

Subtraction: Take From

_____   _____
- - - - - - - -   - - - - - - - -

_____   **take away**   _____

_____
- - - - - - - -
_____

DIRECTIONS 1. Tell a subtraction word problem about the children. Write the number that shows how many children in all. Write the number that shows how many children are leaving. Write the number that shows how many children are left.

Name _____

Lesson 47
COMMON CORE STANDARD CC.K.OA.1
Lesson Objective: Use expressions to represent subtraction.

Subtraction: Take Apart

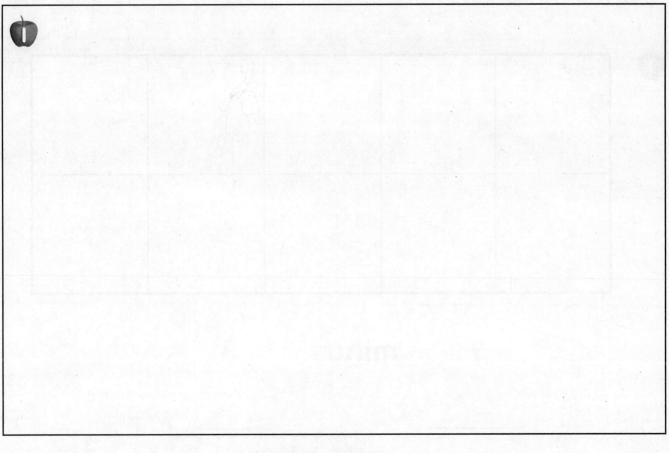

7 minus 2

DIRECTIONS   I. Henry has seven counters. Place seven red counters in the workspace. Trace the number 7 to show how many in all. Two of Henry's counters are yellow. Turn two of the counters to the yellow side. Trace the number 2. How many of Henry's counters are red? Count the red counters. Trace the number 5. Trace and color the counters you placed.

Operations and Algebraic Thinking

Subtraction: Take Apart

1.

9   minus   3

_____   _____

_ _ _ _ _   **_ _ _**   _ _ _ _ _

_____   _____

_____

_ _ _ _ _

_____

DIRECTIONS   1. Listen to the subtraction word problem. Jane has
nine counters. Three of her counters are red. The rest of her counters
are yellow. How many are yellow? Place nine counters in the ten
frame. Draw and color the counters. Write the number that shows
how many in all. Write the number that shows how many are red.
Write the number that shows how many are yellow.

Name _____

Problem Solving • Act Out Subtraction Problems

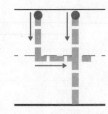 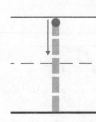 

DIRECTIONS   Listen to and act out the subtraction word problems.
1. There are four children sitting on the floor. Trace the number 4. Then one child leaves. Trace the number 1. How many children are sitting on the floor now? Trace the number 3 to show how many children are left. **2.** There are three children at the table. Then two children walk away. Write the number that shows how many children are left. Trace to complete the subtraction sentence.

Operations and Algebraic Thinking

Problem Solving • Act Out Subtraction Problems

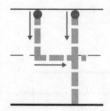

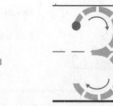

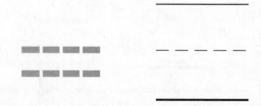

DIRECTIONS **1.** Tell a subtraction word problem about the beavers. Trace the numbers and the symbols. Write the number that shows how many beavers are left. **2.** Draw to show what you know about the subtraction sentence. Write how many are left. Tell a friend about your drawing.

Algebra • Write More
Addition Sentences

DIRECTIONS There were some frogs. Five more frogs come. Then there were seven frogs. How many frogs were there before? **1.** Circle the frogs being added. Trace the number. How many frogs are in the set to start with? Write the number. **2.** How many frogs are there now? Write the number. **3.** Trace the numbers and symbols to show this as an addition sentence.

Algebra • Write More
Addition Sentences

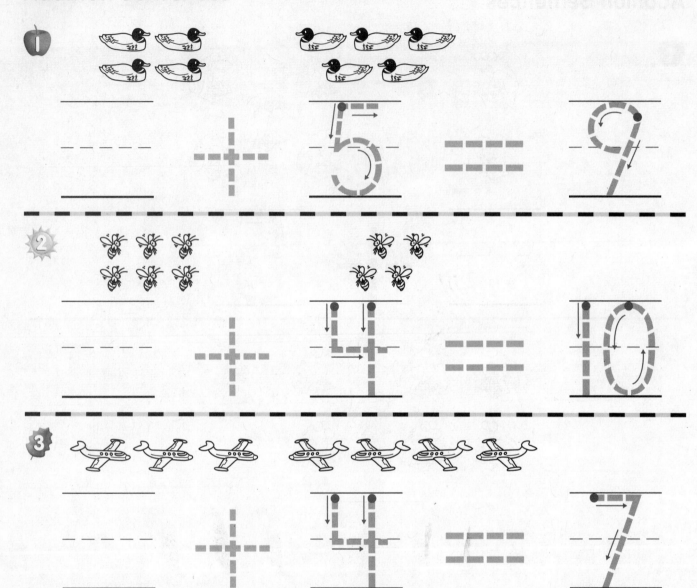

DIRECTIONS 1–4. Tell an addition word problem. Circle the set being added. How many are in the set to start with? Write and trace to complete the addition sentence.

Lesson **50**

COMMON CORE STANDARD CC.K.OA.2
Lesson Objective: Solve subtraction word problems within 10 and record the equation.

Algebra • Write More Subtraction Sentences

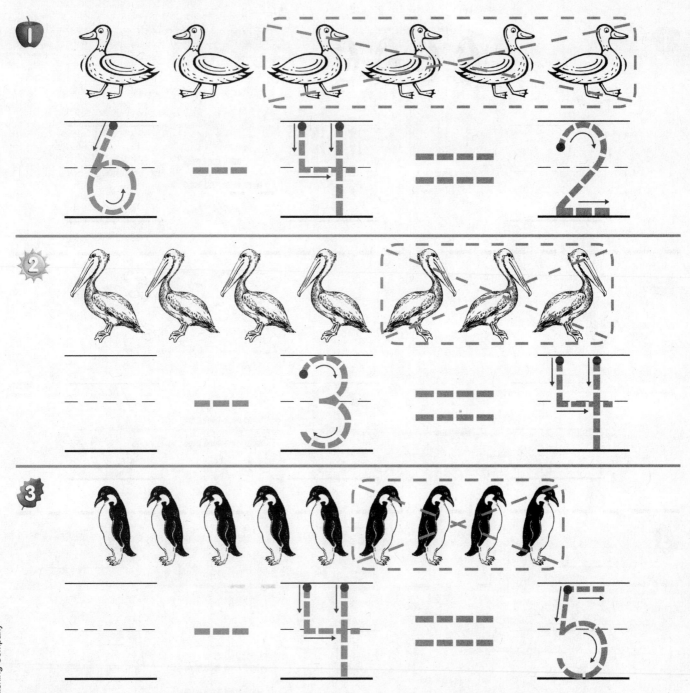

DIRECTIONS   **I.** Listen to the subtraction word problem. Some ducks are sitting. Four ducks leave. There are two ducks left. How many ducks are there to start with? Count the entire set to find how many ducks there are to start with. Trace the number. Then trace the circle and X to show how many are being taken from the set. Trace to complete the subtraction sentence.   **2–3.** Tell a subtraction word problem about the birds. Count the entire set to find how many there are to start with. Write and trace to complete the subtraction sentence.

Operations and Algebraic Thinking

Algebra • Write More
Subtraction Sentences

🍎 1

_ _ _ _ _   −   _ _ _ 4   =   _ _ _ 3

- -

2

_ _ _ _   −   _ _ 3   =   _ _ 6

- -

3

_ _ _ _ _   −   _ _ 1   =   _ _ 5

DIRECTIONS   1–3. Listen to a subtraction word problem about the birds. There are
some birds. _____ birds are taken from the set. Draw more birds to show how many
you started with. How many birds did you start with? Write the number to complete the
subtraction sentence.

100

Name _____

Lesson 51
COMMON CORE STANDARD CC.K.OA.2
Lesson Objective: Understand addition
as putting together or adding to and subtraction
as taking apart or taking from to solve word
problems.

Algebra • Addition and Subtraction

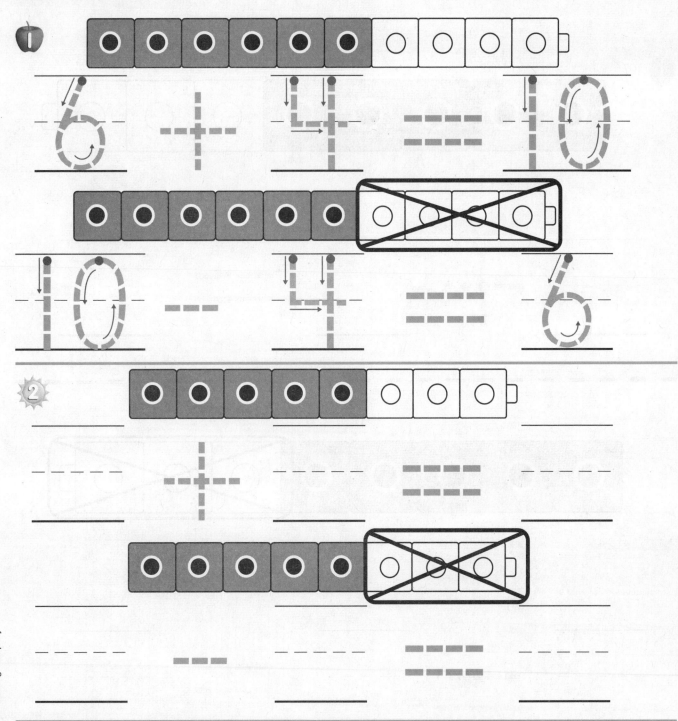

© Houghton Mifflin Harcourt Publishing Company

DIRECTIONS   1. Listen to the addition and subtraction word problems. Use cubes to add and to subtract. Complete the number sentences. Max has six blue cubes. Then he finds four yellow cubes. How many cubes does he have in all? Max has ten cubes. Then he gives four cubes to a friend. How many cubes does he have now?   **2.** Tell addition and subtraction word problems. Use cubes to add and to subtract. Complete the number sentences.

Operations and Algebraic Thinking

101

Algebra • Addition and Subtraction

 1

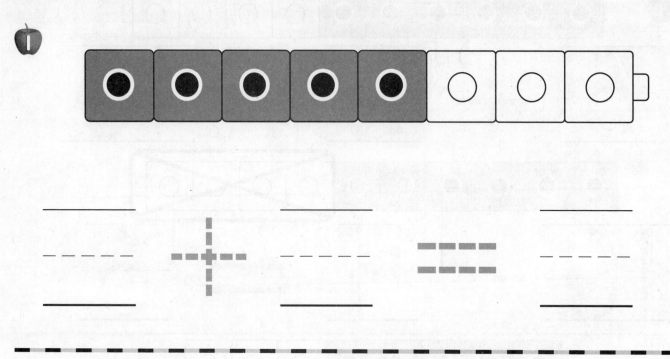

___ ___ + ___ ___ = ___ ___

2

___ ___ ___ ___ = ___ ___ ___

DIRECTIONS 1–2. Tell an addition or subtraction word problem. Use cubes to add or subtract. Complete the number sentence.

102

Lesson 52

COMMON CORE STANDARD CC.K.OA.3
Lesson Objective: Use objects or drawings to decompose 5 into pairs in more than one way.

Algebra • Ways to Make 5

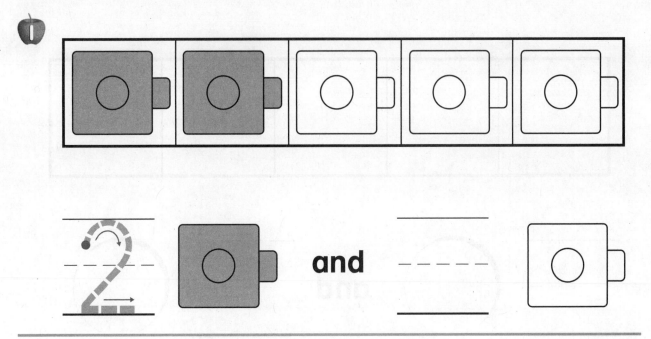

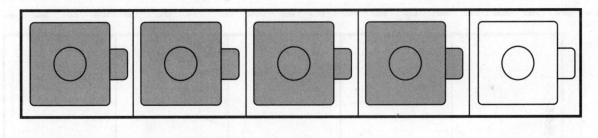

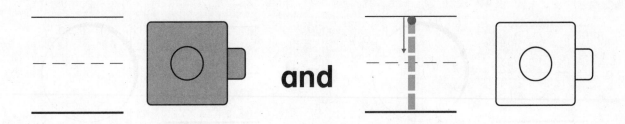

DIRECTIONS 1. Count the gray cubes in the five frame. Trace the number. Count the white cubes in the five frame. Write the number to show a way to make 5. **2.** Count the gray cubes in the five frame. Write the number. Count the white cubes in the five frame. Trace the number to show a way to make 5.

Operations and Algebraic Thinking

Algebra • Ways to Make 5

1

_____
- - - - - - -
_____   ◯   **and**   _____
- - - - - - -
_____   ◯

- -

2

_____
- - - - - - -
_____   ◯   **and**   _____   ◯
- - - - - - -
_____

DIRECTIONS   1–2. Use two colors of counters to show a way to make 5. Color to show the counters. Write the numbers to show the pair that makes 5.

Name _____

Lesson 53
COMMON CORE STANDARD CC.K.OA.3
Lesson Objective: Decompose numbers within 5 into pairs in more than one way and record each decomposition with an equation.

Algebra • Number Pairs to 5

1
$$5 = \quad \square + 4$$

2
$$5 = \quad 2 + \quad$$

3
$$5 = \quad 3 + \quad$$

4
$$5 = \quad 4 + \quad$$

DIRECTIONS Use two-color counters.   **1–4.** Place five yellow counters in a row as shown. Look at the gray number. Turn that many counters to red. How many counters are yellow? Trace or write the numbers to show a number pair that makes 5.

Operations and Algebraic Thinking

Algebra • Number Pairs to 5

1 **3** = ___ ___ + ___ ___

2 **4** = ___ ___ + ___ ___

3 **5** = ___ ___ + ___ ___

DIRECTIONS 1–3. Look at the number at the beginning of the addition sentence. Place two colors of cubes on the cube train to show a number pair for that number. Complete the addition sentence to show a number pair. Color the cube train to match the addition sentence.

Name _____

Algebra · Number Pairs
for 6 and 7

 1

$$6 = 1 + 5$$

 2

$$6 = 3 + \underline{}$$

3

$$7 = 5 + \underline{}$$

DIRECTIONS Use two-color counters. **1–2.** Place six yellow counters in a row as shown. Look at the gray number. Turn that many counters to red. How many counters are yellow? Trace or write the numbers to show a number pair that makes 6. **3.** Place seven yellow counters in a row as shown. Look at the gray number. Turn that many counters to red. How many counters are yellow? Trace or write the numbers to show a number pair that makes 7.

Operations and Algebraic Thinking

Name _____

Algebra • Number Pairs for 6 and 7

1

6 = ____ + ____

2

7 = ____ + ____

DIRECTIONS 1–2. Look at the number at the beginning of the addition sentence. Place two colors of cubes on the cube train to show a number pair for that number. Complete the addition sentence to show a number pair. Color the cube train to match the addition sentence.

Lesson 55

COMMON CORE STANDARD CC.K.OA.3

Lesson Objective: Decompose 8 into pairs in more than one way and record each decomposition with an equation.

Algebra • Number Pairs for 8

1 $8 = 1 + 7$

2 $8 = 2 + \underline{}$

3 $8 = 3 + \underline{}$

4 $8 = 4 + \underline{}$

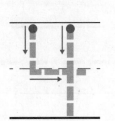 

DIRECTIONS Use two-color counters.   **1–4.** Place eight yellow counters in a row as shown. Look at the gray number. Turn that many counters to red. How many counters are yellow? Trace or write the numbers to show a number pair that makes 8.

Operations and Algebraic Thinking

Name _____

Algebra • Number Pairs for 8

1

8 = ___ + ___

2

8 = ___ + ___

3

8 = ___ + ___

4

8 = ___ + ___

DIRECTIONS Use two colors of cubes to make a cube train to show the number pairs that make 8. **1–4.** Complete the addition sentence to show a number pair for 8. Color the cube train to match the addition sentence in Exercise 4.

110

Algebra • Number Pairs for 9

1 $9 = \underline{\qquad}$ 1 + 8

2 $9 = \underline{\qquad}$ 2 + __

3 $9 = \underline{\qquad}$ 3 + __

4 $9 = \underline{\qquad}$ 4 + __

DIRECTIONS Use two-color counters.   **1–4.** Place nine yellow counters in a row as shown. Look at the gray number. Turn that many counters to red. How many counters are yellow? Trace or write the numbers to show a number pair that makes 9.

Operations and Algebraic Thinking

Name _____

Algebra • Number Pairs for 9

1

9 $=$ _____ $+$ _____

2

9 $=$ _____ $+$ _____

3

9 $=$ _____ $+$ _____

4

9 $=$ _____ $+$ _____

DIRECTIONS Use two colors of cubes to make a cube train to show the number pairs that make 9. **1–4.** Complete the addition sentence to show a number pair for 9. Color the cube train to match the addition sentence in Exercise 4.

Name _____

Algebra · Number Pairs for 10

1   10 = 1 + 9

  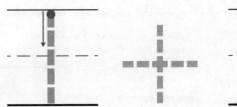

2   10 = 2 + ___

 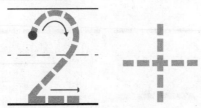

3   10 = 3 + ___

 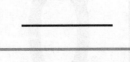

4   10 = 4 + ___

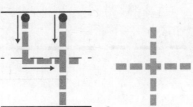 

DIRECTIONS   Use two-color counters. **1–4.** Place ten yellow counters in a row as shown. Look at the gray number. Turn that many counters to red. How many counters are yellow? Trace or write the numbers to show a number pair that makes 10.

Algebra • Number Pairs for 10

1 $10 = $ ____ + ____

2 $10 = $ ____ + ____

3 $10 = $ ____ + ____

4 $10 = $ ____ + ____

DIRECTIONS Use two colors of cubes to build a cube train to show the number pairs that make 10. **1–4.** Complete the addition sentence to show a number pair for 10. Color the cube train to match the addition sentence in Exercise 4.

Algebra • Ways to Make 10

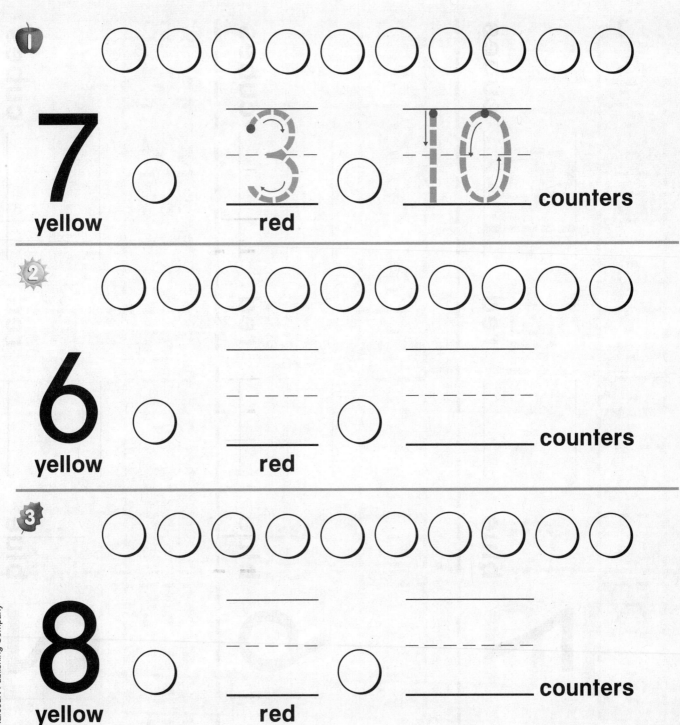

1.

7 yellow   ○   **3** red   ○   **10** counters

2.

6 yellow   ○   _____ red   ○   _____ counters

3.

8 yellow   ○   _____ red   ○   _____ counters

DIRECTIONS 1. Look at the first number. Color that many counters yellow. Color the rest of the counters red. Trace the numbers. **2–3.** Look at the first number. Color that many counters yellow. Color the rest of the counters red. Write how many red counters. Write how many counters in all.

Operations and Algebraic Thinking

Name _____

Algebra • Ways to Make 10

1

7

blue

red

cubes

2

6

blue

red

cubes

3

2

blue

red

cubes

DIRECTIONS 1–3. Use blue to color the cubes to match the number. Use red to color the other cubes. Write how many red cubes. Trace or write the number that shows how many cubes in all.

Name _____

Algebra • Write Addition Sentences for 10

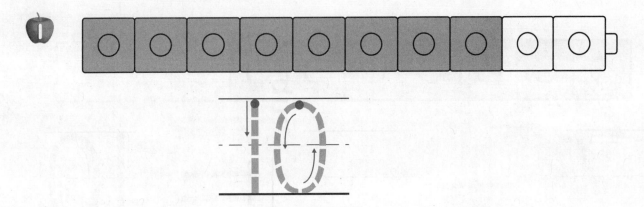

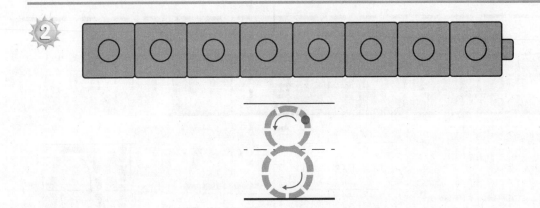

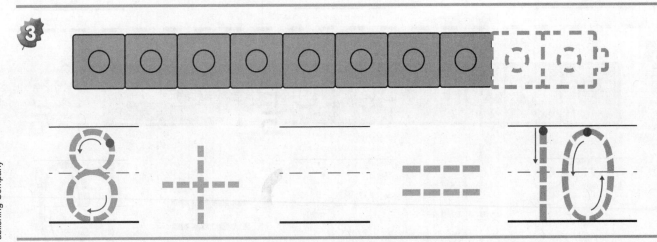

DIRECTIONS **1.** Count the number of cubes. How many are there? Trace the number. **2.** How many gray cubes? Draw a dot on each gray cube as you count. Trace the number. **3.** How many white cubes do you need to make 10? Trace each white cube as you count. Write and trace to show this as an addition sentence.

Operations and Algebraic Thinking

Algebra • Write Addition
Sentences for 10

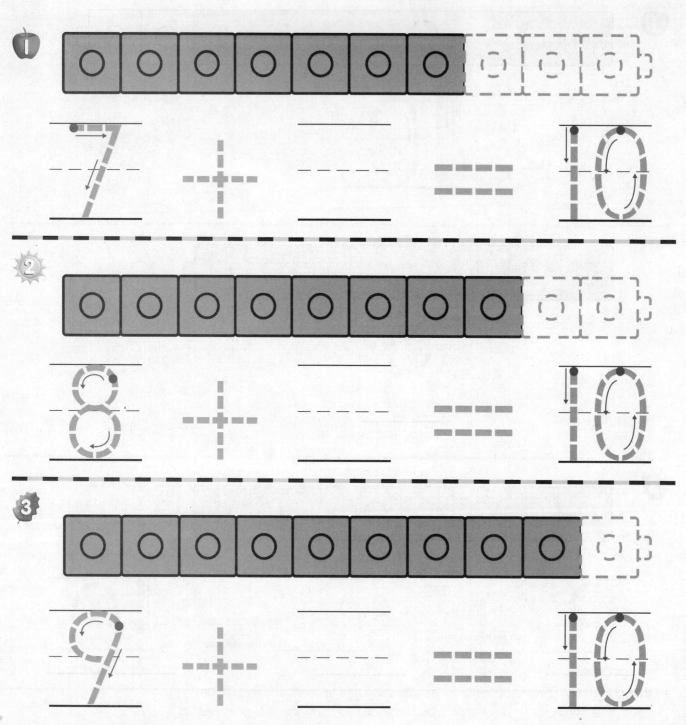

1 7 + ___ = 10

2 8 + ___ = 10

3 9 + ___ = 10

DIRECTIONS 1–3. Look at the cube train. How many gray cubes do you see? How many blue cubes do you need to add to make 10? Use blue to color those cubes. Write and trace to show this as an addition sentence.

Name _____

Lesson 60

COMMON CORE STANDARD CC.K.OA.5
Lesson Objective: Use objects and drawings to solve addition word problems within 5.

Algebra · Model and Draw Addition Problems

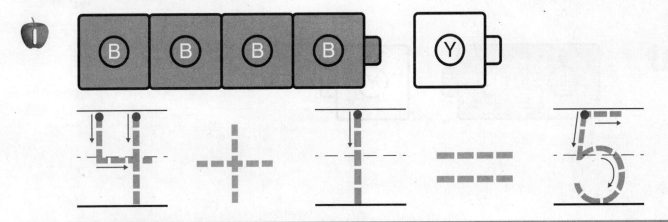

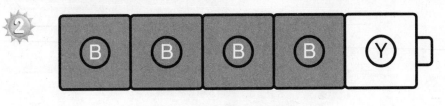

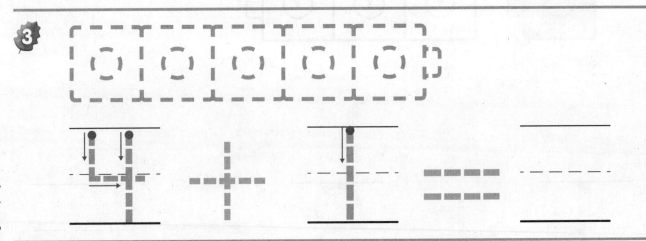

DIRECTIONS Emma has four blue cubes and one yellow cube. How many cubes does she have? **1.** Place cubes as shown to show the sets of cubes. Count how many in each set. Trace the numbers and the symbol. **2.** Place cubes as shown to model the cubes put together. Count the cubes. Write the number. **3.** Trace the cube train. Color to show the cubes put together. Trace and write to complete the addition sentence.

Operations and Algebraic Thinking

Algebra • Model and Draw
Addition Problems

 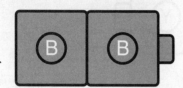 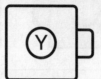

  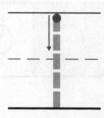 

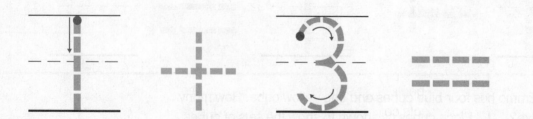

DIRECTIONS 1–2. Place cubes as shown. B is for blue, and Y is for yellow. Tell an addition word problem. Model to show the cubes put together. Draw the cube train. Trace and write to complete the addition sentence.

120

© Houghton Mifflin Harcourt Publishing Company

Algebra • Write Addition Sentences

$$3 + \_\_\_ = \_\_\_$$

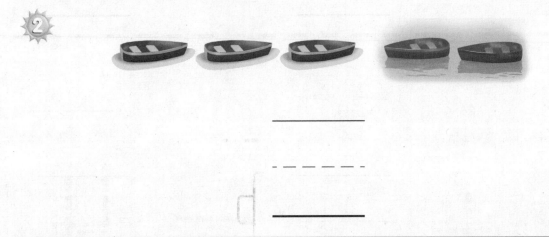

$$\_\_\_\_\_ = \_\_\_\_\_$$

$$3 + 2 = 5$$

DIRECTIONS There are three boats. Some more boats come. Now there are five boats. How many more boats come?   **1.** Circle the boats you start with. Trace the number. How many boats are being added to the set? Write the number.   **2.** How many boats are there now? Write the number.   **3.** Trace the numbers and symbols to show this as an addition sentence.

Operations and Algebraic Thinking

Algebra • Write Addition Sentences

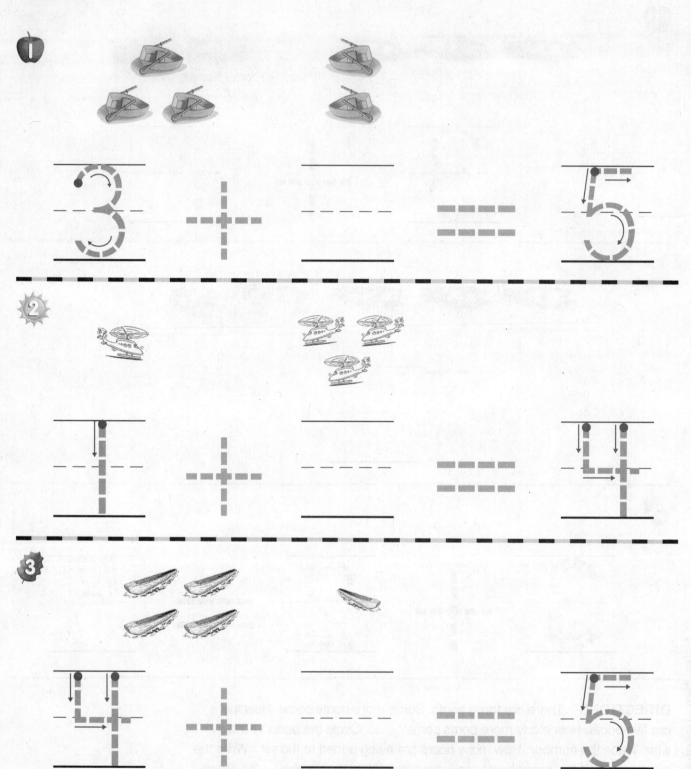

1 3 + ___ = 5

2 1 + ___ = 4

3 4 + ___ = 5

DIRECTIONS 1–3. Tell an addition word problem about the sets.
Circle the set you start with. How many are being added to the set? How
many are there now? Write and trace to complete the addition sentence.

Algebra • Model and Draw
Subtraction Problems

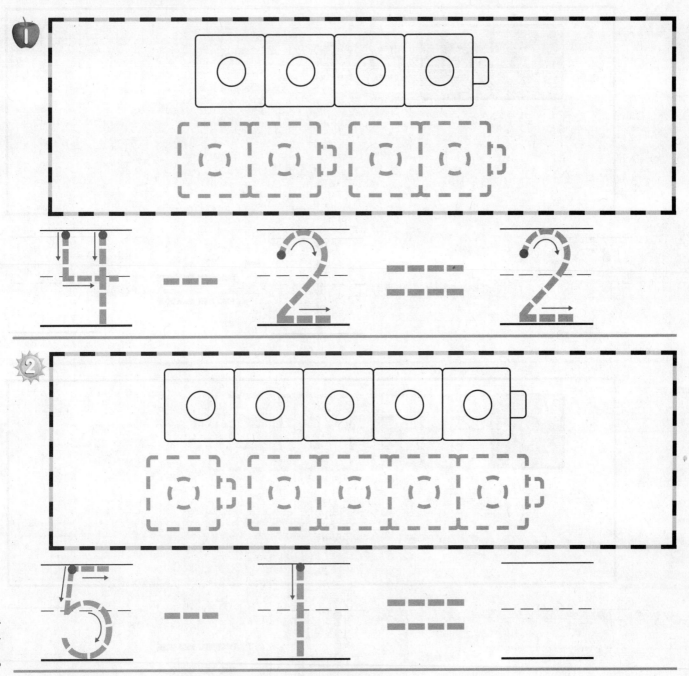

DIRECTIONS Model the subtraction word problem with cubes. **1.** There are four race cars. Two race cars are blue and the rest are green. How many race cars are green? Start with four cubes. Take apart a two-cube train. How many cubes are left? Trace the cube trains. Trace to complete the subtraction sentence. **2.** There are five rockets. One rocket is orange and the rest are red. How many rockets are red? Start with a five-cube train. Take apart one cube. How many cubes are left? Trace the cube trains. Trace and write to complete the subtraction sentence.

Operations and Algebraic Thinking

Algebra • Model and Draw
Subtraction Problems

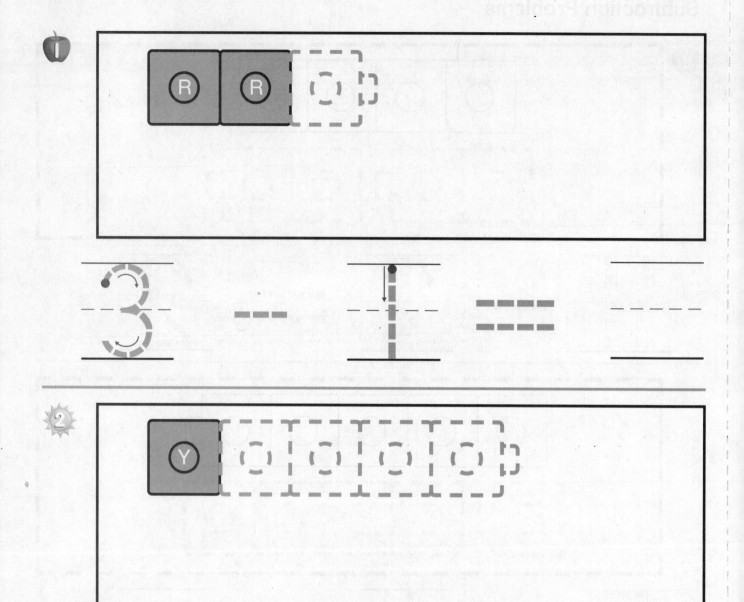

**① **

3 – 1 = ___

**② **

5 – 1 = ___

DIRECTIONS 1. Model a three-cube train. Two cubes are red and the rest are blue. Take apart the cube train to show how many cubes are blue. Draw and color the cube trains. Trace and write to complete the subtraction sentence. 2. Model a five-cube train. One cube is yellow and the rest are green. Take apart the train to show how many cubes are green. Draw and color the cube trains. Trace and write to complete the subtraction sentence.

124

Name _____

Lesson 63

COMMON CORE STANDARD CC.K.OA.5

Lesson Objective: Solve subtraction word problems within 5 and record the equation.

Algebra • Write Subtraction Sentences

 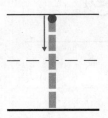 

3 — 1 = 2

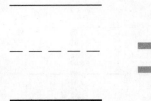

4 — ___ = 2

5 — ___ = 2

DIRECTIONS 1. Listen to the subtraction word problem. I saw three dolphins. Some swam away. Then there were only two. How many dolphins swam away? Trace the circle and X to show one dolphin is being taken from the set. Trace to complete the subtraction sentence. **2–3.** Tell what is happening. Trace the circle and X to show how many are being taken from the set. Trace and write to complete the subtraction sentence.

Algebra • Write Subtraction Sentences

1

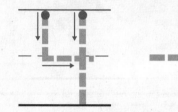 —  = _____

2

 — 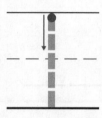 = _____

3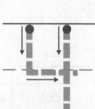

DIRECTIONS 1–3. Listen to the subtraction word problem about the animals. There are ____ ____. Some are taken from the set. Now there are ____. How many were taken from the set? Circle and mark an X to show how many are being taken from the set. Trace and write to complete the subtraction sentence.

Model and Count 11 and 12

11
eleven

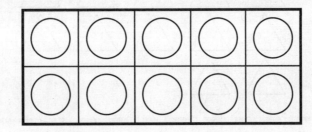

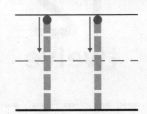

12
twelve

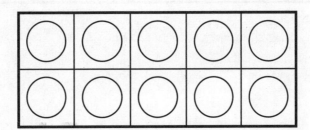

DIRECTIONS **1.** How many counters are in the ten frame? Draw a dot on each counter as you count. Trace the counter below to show 11. Trace the number. **2.** How many counters are in the ten frame? Draw a dot on each counter as you count. Draw counters below to show 12. Write the number.

Number and Operations in Base Ten

Model and Count 11 and 12

 12
twelve

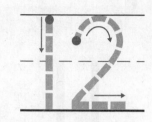

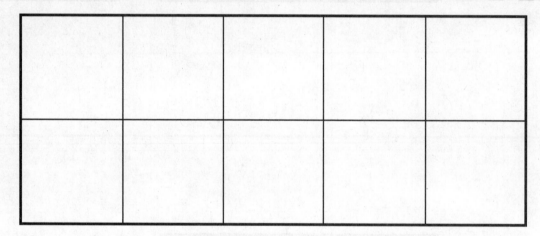

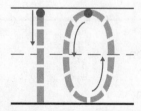 **ones and** _____ **ones**

DIRECTIONS 1. Count and tell how many. Trace the number. 2. Use counters to show the number 12. Draw the counters. 3. Look at the counters you drew. How many ones are in the ten frame? Trace the number. How many more ones are there? Write the number.

128

Model and Count 13 and 14

13
thirteen

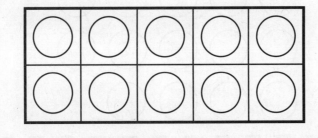

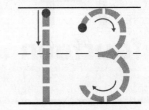

②

14
fourteen

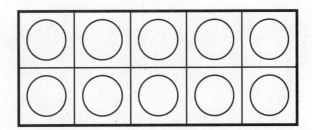

DIRECTIONS 1. How many counters in the ten frame? Draw a dot on each counter as you count. Trace the counters below to show 13. Trace the number. 2. How many counters in the ten frame? Draw a dot on each counter as you count. Draw counters below to show 14. Write the number.

Number and Operations in Base Ten

Model and Count 13 and 14

14
fourteen

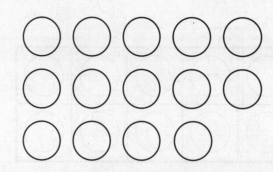

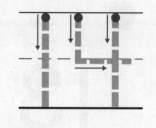

---

②

---

③ 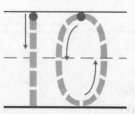 10 _____ ones and _____ ones

---

DIRECTIONS 1. Count and tell how many. Trace the number. **2.** Use counters to show the number 14. Draw the counters. **3.** Look at the counters you drew. How many ones are in the ten frame? Trace the number. How many more ones are there? Write the number.

Model, Count, and Write 15

15
fifteen

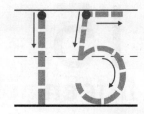

_____

- - - - - - -

_____

_____

- - - - - - -

_____

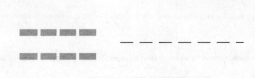

DIRECTIONS   I. Count and tell how many. Draw a dot on each object as you count. Trace the number.   2. Look at the objects in the ten frame in Exercise I. Count and write the number.   3. Look at the objects below the ten frame in Exercise I. Count and write the number.   4. Look at the ten ones and some more ones in Exercise I. Complete the addition sentence to match.

Number and Operations in Base Ten

Model, Count, and Write 15

15
fifteen

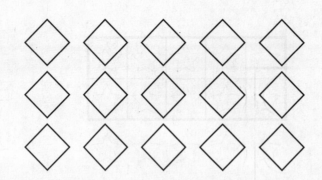

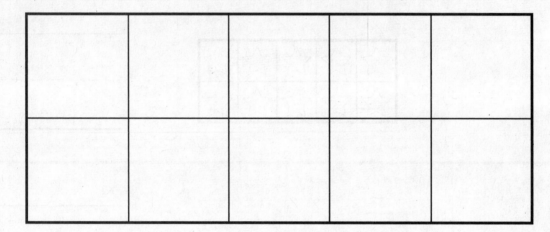

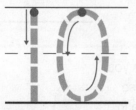 _____ ones and _____ ones

DIRECTIONS **1.** Count and tell how many. Trace the number. **2.** Use counters to show the number 15. Draw the counters. **3.** Look at the counters you drew. How many ones are in the ten frame? Trace the number. How many more ones? Write the number.

132

Model and Count 16 and 17

Lesson 67

COMMON CORE STANDARD CC.K.NBT.1

Lesson Objective: Use objects to decompose the numbers 16 and 17 into ten ones and some further ones.

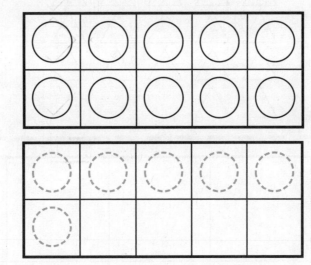

16
sixteen

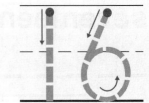

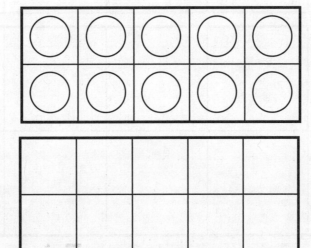

17
seventeen

DIRECTIONS   **1.** How many counters are in the top ten frame? Draw a dot on each counter as you count. Trace the counters in the ten frame below to show 16. Trace the number.   **2.** How many counters are in the top ten frame? Draw a dot on each counter as you count. Draw counters in the ten frame below to show 17. Write the number.

Number and Operations in Base Ten

Name _____

Model and Count 16 and 17

17
seventeen

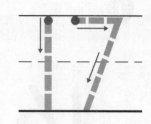

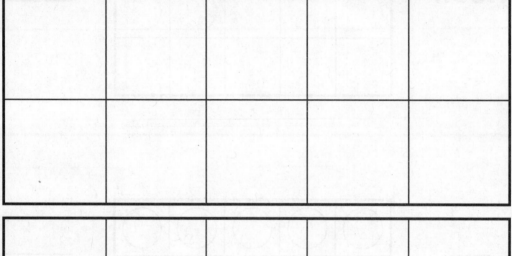

 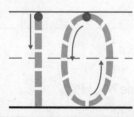 ones and _____ ones

DIRECTIONS 1. Count and tell how many. Trace the number. **2.** Place counters in the ten frames to show the number 17. Draw the counters. **3.** Look at the counters you drew in the ten frames. How many ones are in the top ten frame? Trace the number. How many ones are in the bottom ten frame? Write the number.

Lesson 68

COMMON CORE STANDARD CC.K.NBT.1
Lesson Objective: Use objects to decompose the numbers 18 and 19 into ten ones and some further ones.

Model and Count 18 and 19

18
eighteen

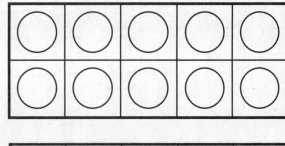

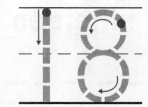

19
nineteen

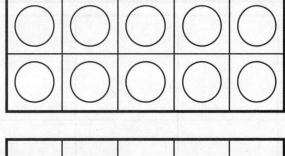

DIRECTIONS **1.** How many counters are in the top ten frame? Draw a dot on each counter as you count. Trace the counters in the ten frame below to show 18. Trace the number. **2.** How many counters are in the top ten frame? Draw a dot on each counter as you count. Draw counters in the ten frame to show 19. Write the number.

Number and Operations in Base Ten

Name _____

Model and Count 18 and 19

 19
nineteen

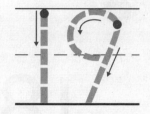

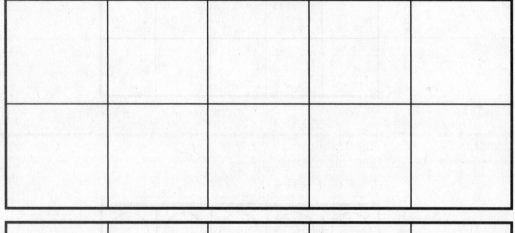

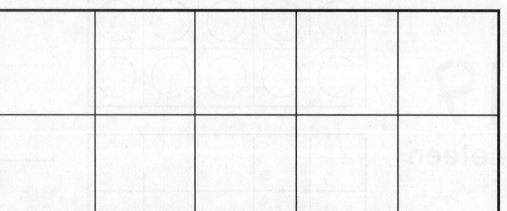

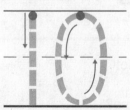 **ones and** _____ **ones**

DIRECTIONS 1. Count and tell how many. Trace the number. 2. Place counters in the ten frame to show the number 19. Draw the counters. 3. Look at the counters you drew in the ten frames. How many ones are in the top ten frame? Trace the number. How many ones are in the bottom ten frame? Write the numbers.

Length, Height, and Weight

DIRECTIONS 1. Use red to trace the line that shows how to measure the length. 2. Use blue to trace the line that shows how to measure the height. 3–4. Use red to trace the line that shows how to measure the length. Use blue to trace the line that shows how to measure the height. Talk about another way to measure the object.

Measurement and Data

Name _____

Length, Height, and Weight

DIRECTIONS 1–4. Use red to trace the line that shows how to measure the length. Use blue to trace the line that shows how to measure the height. Talk about another way to measure the object.

138

Name _____

Lesson 70
COMMON CORE STANDARD CC.K.MD.2
Lesson Objective: Directly compare the lengths of two objects.

Compare Lengths

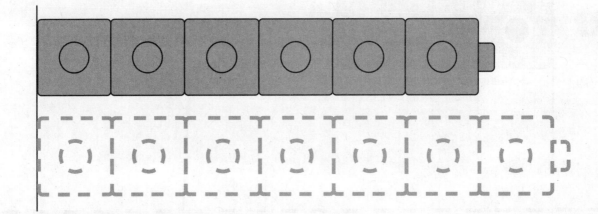

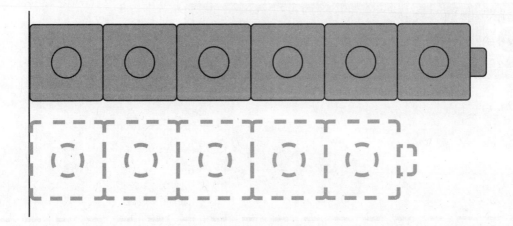

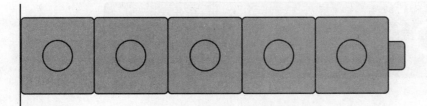

DIRECTIONS **1.** Place cubes on the longer cube train. Trace and color the cube train. **2.** Place cubes on the shorter cube train. Trace and color the cube train. **3.** Make a cube train that is longer than the cube train shown. Draw and color the cube train.

Measurement and Data

Name _____

Compare Lengths

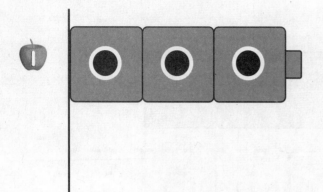

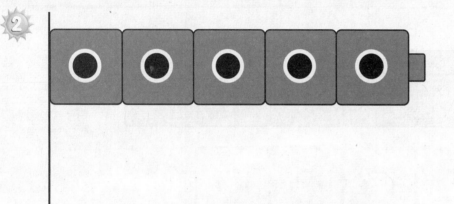

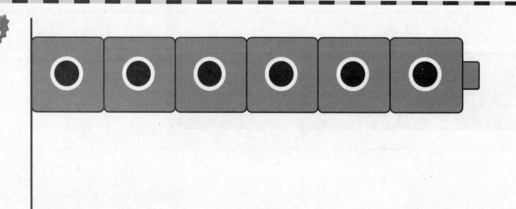

DIRECTIONS **1.** Make a cube train that is longer than the cube train shown. Draw and color the cube train. **2.** Make a cube train that is shorter than the cube train shown. Draw and color the cube train. **3.** Make a cube train that is about the same length as the cube train shown. Draw and color the cube train.

Name _____

Compare Heights

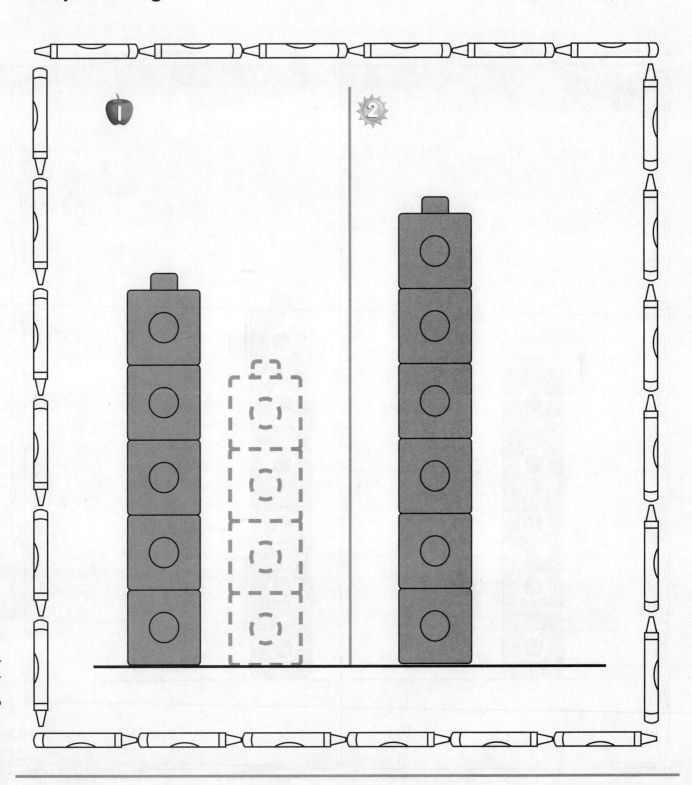

DIRECTIONS 1. Place cubes on the shorter cube tower. Trace and color the cube tower. 2. Make a cube tower that is taller than the cube tower shown. Draw and color the cube tower.

Measurement and Data

Compare Heights

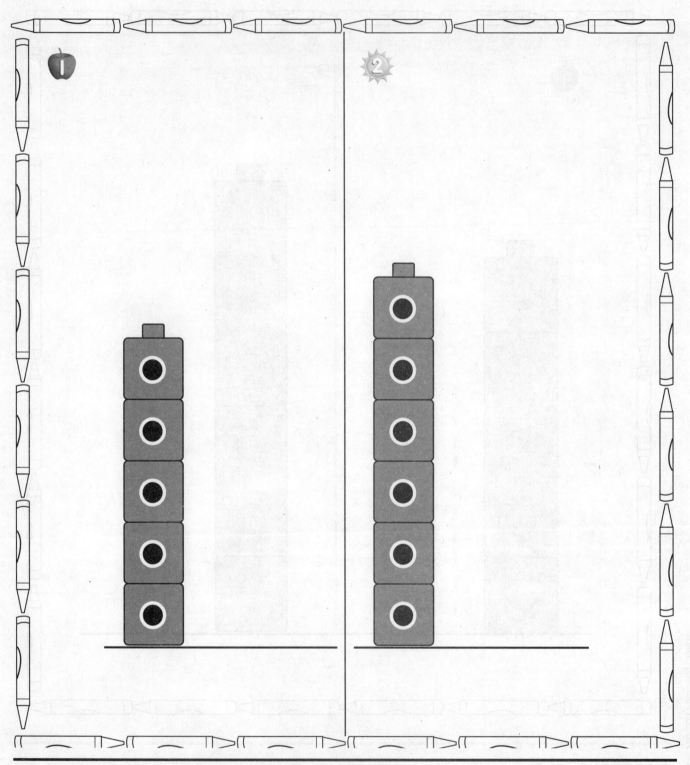

DIRECTIONS **1.** Make a cube tower that is taller than the cube tower shown. Draw and color the cube tower. **2.** Make a cube tower that is shorter than the cube tower shown. Draw and color the cube tower.

Name _____

Lesson 72
COMMON CORE STANDARD CC.K.MD.2
Lesson Objective: Solve problems by using the strategy *draw a picture*.

Problem Solving • Direct Comparison

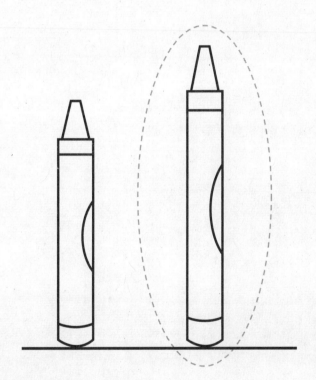

DIRECTIONS   **1.** Compare the two objects by height. See which one goes higher. Say *taller than*, *shorter than*, or about the *same height* to describe the objects. Trace around the taller object.   **2.** Find two small classroom objects. Place one end of each object on the line. Compare the heights. Draw the objects. Say *taller than*, *shorter than*, or *about the same height* to describe the heights. Circle the shorter object.

Measurement and Data

Problem Solving • Direct Comparison

DIRECTIONS **1.** Find two small classroom objects. Place one end of each object on the line. Compare the lengths. Draw the objects. Say *longer than, shorter than,* or *about the same length* to describe the lengths. Circle the longer object. **2.** Find two small classroom objects. Place one end of each object on the line. Compare the heights. Draw the objects. Say *taller than, shorter than,* or *about the same height* to describe the heights. Circle the shorter object.

Compare Weights

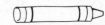

DIRECTIONS 1–4. Find the objects. Hold one in each hand. Circle the object that is heavier. Mark an X on the object that is lighter.

Measurement and Data

Name _____

Compare Weights

left   **right**

①

②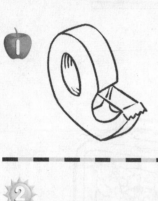

③

④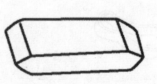

DIRECTIONS Find the first object in the row, and hold it in your left hand. Find the rest of the objects in the row, and hold each object in your right hand. **1–2.** Circle the object that is lighter than the object in your left hand. **3–4.** Circle the object that is heavier than the object in your left hand.

Algebra • Classify and Count by Color

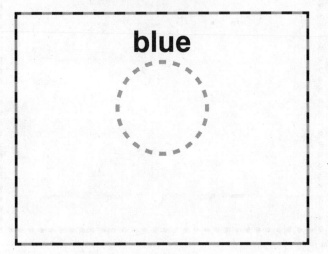

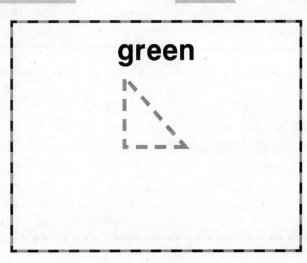

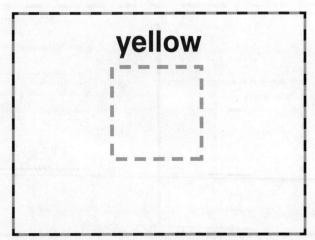

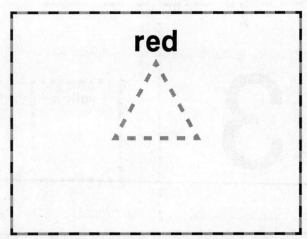

DIRECTIONS 1. Place a green triangle, red triangle, blue circle, yellow square, blue rectangle, red rectangle, and green triangle at the top of the page as shown. Sort and classify the shapes by the category of color. Trace and color a shape in each category. Draw and color the rest of the shapes.

Measurement and Data

Algebra • Classify and Count by Color

yellow	red

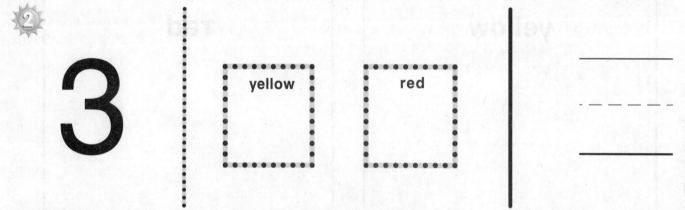

3 | yellow | red | _____

___ - - - ___

_____

DIRECTIONS 1. Place a yellow square, red triangle, red rectangle, yellow square, and red triangle at the top of the page as shown. Sort and classify the shapes by the category of color. Draw and color the shapes in each category. **2.** Look at the categories in Exercise 1. Count how many in each category. Circle the category that has 3 shapes. Write the number.

Algebra • Classify and Count by Shape

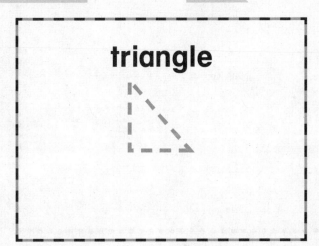

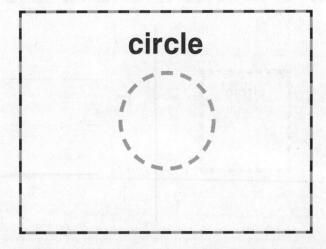

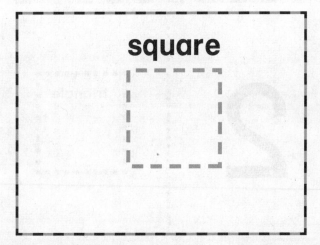

rectangle

triangle

circle

square

DIRECTIONS Place a green triangle, red triangle, blue circle, yellow square, blue rectangle, red rectangle, and green triangle at the top of the page as shown. Sort and classify the shapes by the category of shape. Trace and color a shape in each category. Drawn and color the rest of the shapes.

Measurement and Data

Algebra • Classify and Count by Shape

triangle	circle

② 2 | triangle | circle | _____

_ _ _ _ _ _

_____

DIRECTIONS 1. Place a green triangle, blue circle, red triangle and blue circle at the top of the page as shown. Sort and classify the shapes by the category of shape. Draw and color the shapes in each category. **2.** Look at the categories in Exercise 1. Count how many in each category. Circle the categories that have two shapes. Write the number.

150

Name _____

Name _____

Algebra • Classify and Count by Size

big	small

DIRECTIONS Place a green triangle, red triangle, blue circle, yellow square, blue rectangle, red rectangle, and green triangle at the top of the page as shown. Sort and classify the shapes by the category of size. Trace and color a shape in each category. Draw and color the rest of the shapes.

Measurement and Data

151

Algebra • Classify and Count by Size

small	**big**

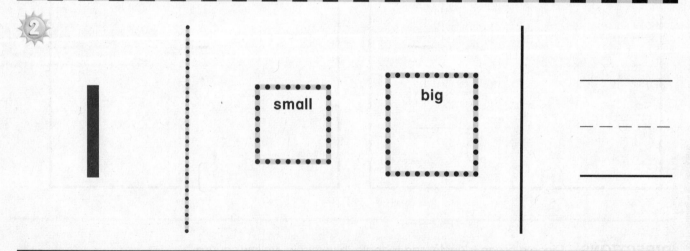

DIRECTIONS **1.** Place a yellow square, blue circle, red rectangle, and blue rectangle at the top of the page as shown. Sort and classify the shapes by the category of size. Draw and color the shapes in each category. **2.** Look at the categories in Exercise 1. Count how many in each category. Circle the category that has one per category. Write the number.

Name _____

Lesson 77
COMMON CORE STANDARD CC.K.MD.3
Lesson Objective: Make a graph to count objects that have been classified into categories.

Make a Concrete Graph

1

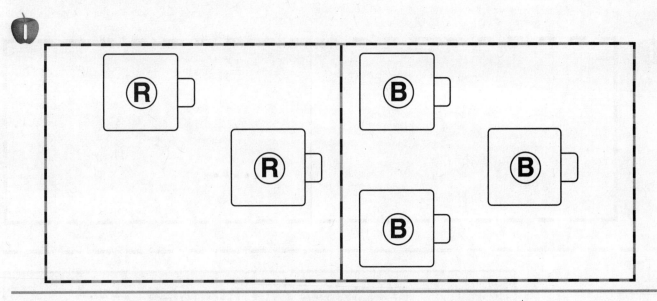

2

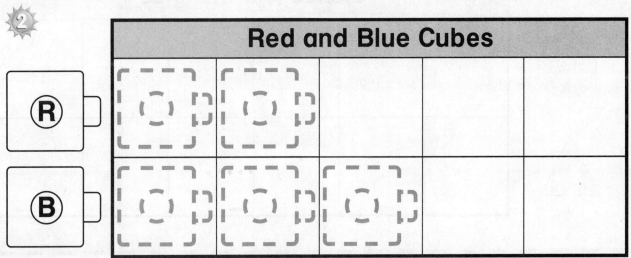

3

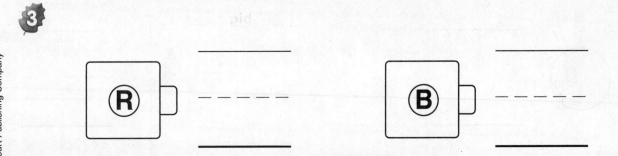

DIRECTIONS **1.** Place cubes in the workspace as shown. R is for red, and B is for blue. See how the cubes are sorted and classified by the category of color. **2.** Move the cubes to the graph. Trace and color the cubes. **3.** Write how many of each cube.

Measurement and Data

Make a Concrete Graph

1

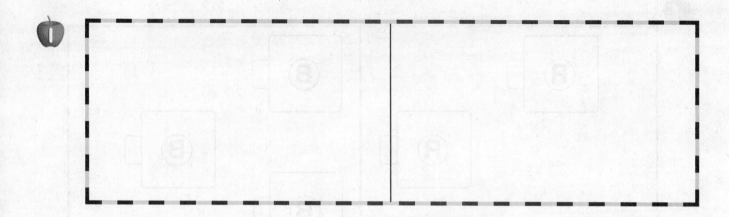

2

Circles and Triangles					
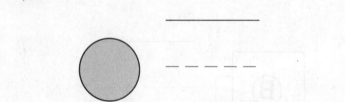						

3

DIRECTIONS **1.** Place a handful of green circles and triangles on the workspace. Sort and classify the shapes by category. **2.** Move the shapes to the graph. Draw and color the shapes. **3.** Write how many of each shape.

Read a Graph

Counter Colors

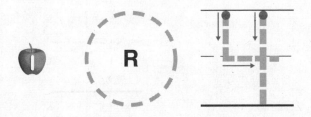

R	R	R	R	R	
Y	Y	Y	Y		

R 4 **Y** _____

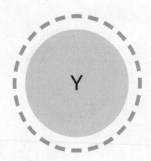

R **Y**

DIRECTIONS 1. Color the counters to show the categories. R is for red, and Y is for yellow. How many counters are in each category? Draw a dot on each counter on the graph as you count. Trace or write the numbers. **2.** Trace the circle around the category that has fewer counters on the graph.

Measurement and Data

Read a Graph

Counter Colors					
 R	R	R	R	R	
Y	Y	Y	Y		

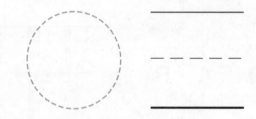

DIRECTIONS **I.** Color the counters to show the categories.
R is for red, and Y is for yellow. How many counters are in each
category? Write the numbers. **2.** Circle the category that has more
counters on the graph.

Lesson 79

COMMON CORE STANDARD CC.K.MD.3

Lesson Objective: Solve problems by using the strategy *use logical reasoning*.

Problem Solving • Sort and Count

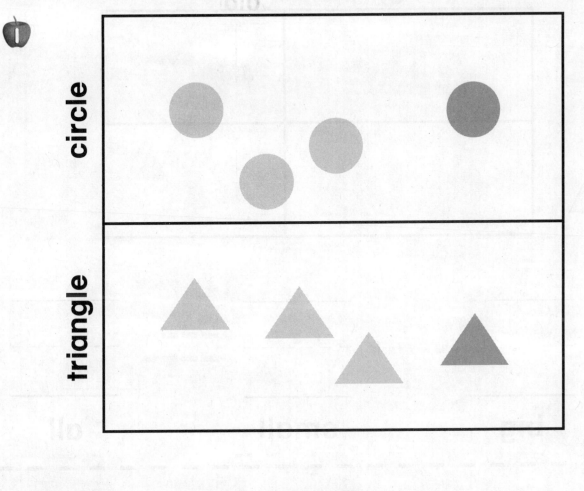

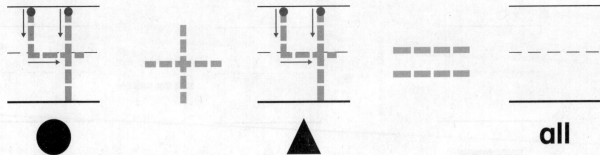

DIRECTIONS I. Look at the sorting mat. How are the shapes sorted? How many circles are there? How many triangles are there? Draw a dot on each shape as you count. Add the two sets. Trace and write the numbers and symbols to complete the addition sentence.

Measurement and Data

Problem Solving • Sort and Count

big　　　　　　**small**

1

___ ___ ___ + ___ ___ ___ **=** ___ ___ ___

big　　　　　　　**small**　　　　　　　**all**

- -

2

___ ___ ___ + ___ ___ ___ **=** ___ ___ ___

all

DIRECTIONS Explain how the shapes are sorted. **1.** How many big and small shapes are shown? Write and trace to complete the addition sentence. **2.** How many rectangles and triangles are shown? Write and trace to complete the addition sentence.

Above and Below

DIRECTIONS **I.** Trace the circle around object that is shaped like a sphere above the bench. Trace the X on the object that is shaped like a cube below the bench.

Geometry

Above and Below

DIRECTIONS **I.** Mark an X on the object that is shaped like a sphere below the table. Circle the object that is shaped like a cube above the table.

Lesson 81

COMMON CORE STANDARD CC.K.G.1

Lesson Objective: Use the terms *beside* and *next to* to describe shapes in the environment.

Name _____

Beside and Next To

DIRECTIONS **1.** Trace the X on the object shaped like a sphere that is next to the object shaped like a cylinder. Trace the circle around the object shaped like a cylinder that is beside the object shaped like a cube.

Geometry

Beside and Next To

DIRECTIONS **I.** Mark an X on the object shaped like a cylinder that is next to the object shaped like a sphere. Circle the object shaped like a cone that is beside the object shaped like a cube. Use the words *next to* and *beside* to name the position of other shapes.

Lesson 82

COMMON CORE STANDARD CC.K.G.1
Lesson Objective: Use the terms *in front of* and *behind* to describe shapes in the environment.

Name _____

In Front Of and Behind

DIRECTIONS **1.** Trace the X on the object shaped like a cube that is behind the object shaped like a cone. Trace the circle around the object shaped like a cone that is in front of the object shaped like a cylinder.

Geometry

In Front Of and Behind

DIRECTIONS   I. Mark an X on the object shaped like a cylinder that is behind the object shaped like a cone. Draw a circle around the object shaped like a cylinder that is in front of the object shaped like a cube. Use the words *in front of* and *behind* to name the position of other shapes.

Identify and Name Circles

DIRECTIONS I. Place a circle on each shaded circle. Color the other circles in the picture.

Geometry

Identify and Name Circles

DIRECTIONS 1. Color the circles in the picture.

Identify and Name Squares

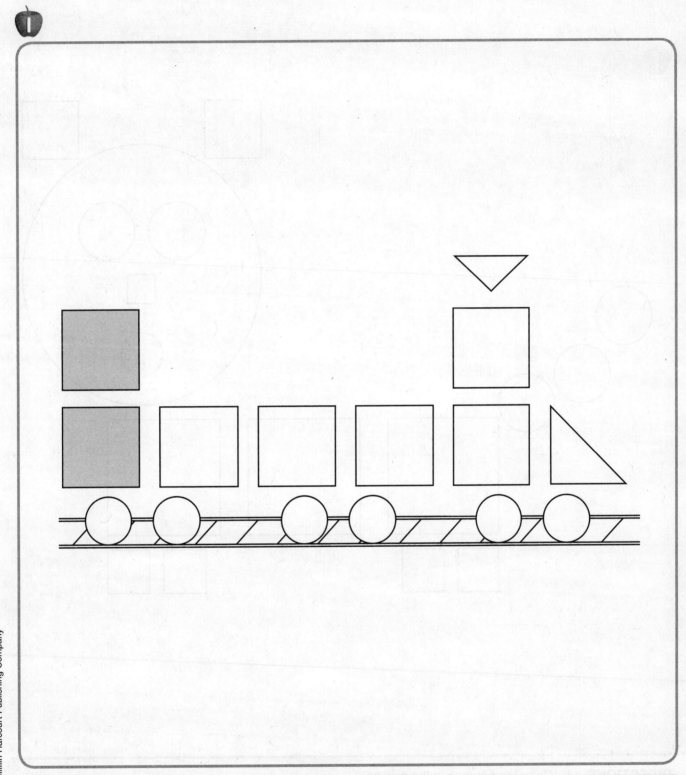

DIRECTIONS 1. Place a square on each shaded square. Color the other squares in the picture.

Geometry

Name _____

Identify and Name Squares

DIRECTIONS **1.** Color the squares in the picture.

Name _____

Lesson 85

COMMON CORE STANDARD CC.K.G.2
Lesson Objective: Identify and name
two-dimensional shapes including triangles.

Identify and Name Triangles

DIRECTIONS **I.** Place a triangle on each shaded triangle. Color the other triangles in the picture.

Geometry

169

Identify and Name Triangles

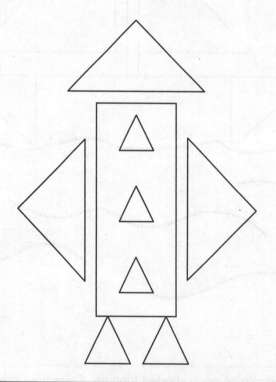

DIRECTIONS 1–2. Color the triangles in the picture.

Lesson 86

COMMON CORE STANDARD CC.K.G.2

Lesson Objective: Identify and name
two-dimensional shapes including rectangles.

Identify and Name Rectangles

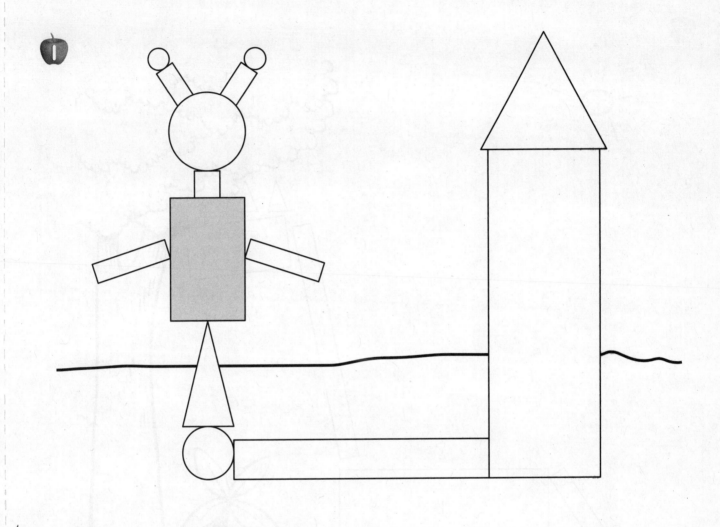

DIRECTIONS **1.** Place a rectangle on the shaded rectangle. Color the other
rectangles in the picture.

Geometry

Identify and Name Rectangles

DIRECTIONS **I.** Color the rectangles in the picture.

Identify and Name Hexagons

Lesson 87

COMMON CORE STANDARD CC.K.G.2

Lesson Objective: Identify and name two-dimensional shapes including hexagons.

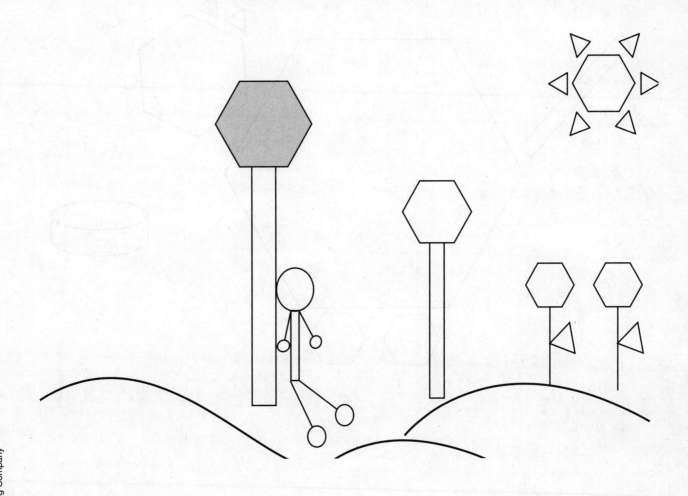

DIRECTIONS 1. Place a hexagon on the shaded hexagon. Color the other hexagons in the picture.

Identify and Name Hexagons

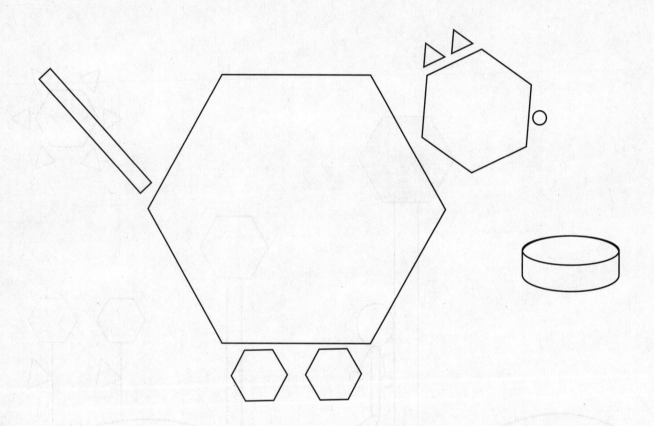

DIRECTIONS **1.** Color the hexagons in the picture.

Lesson 88

COMMON CORE STANDARD CC.K.G.2

Lesson Objective: Identify, name, and describe three-dimensional shapes including spheres.

Identify, Name, and Describe Spheres

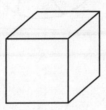

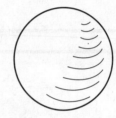

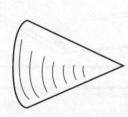

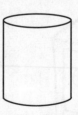

DIRECTIONS   A sphere has a curved surface and no flat surfaces. Use shapes. Trace the shapes with your finger. **1.** Trace the gray sphere with your crayon **2-4.** Color the spheres.

Geometry

Identify, Name, and Describe Spheres

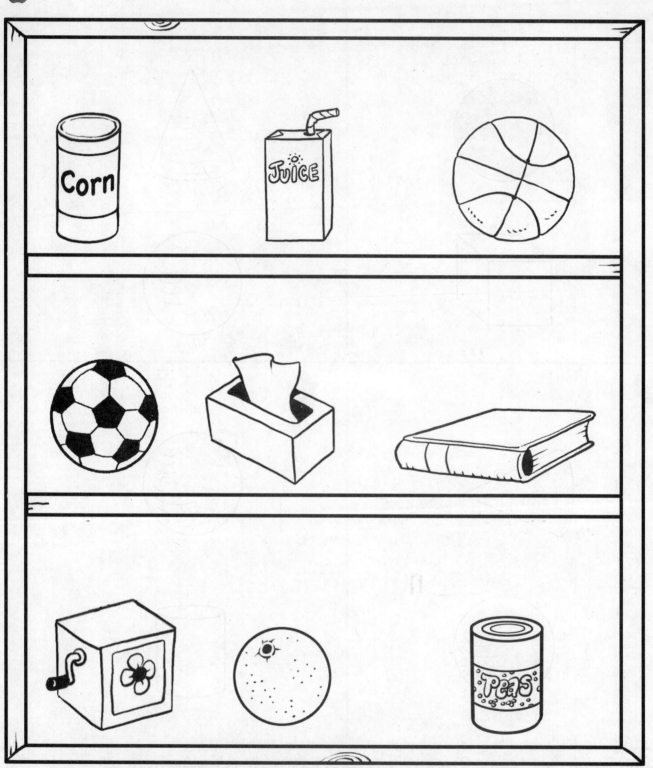

DIRECTIONS   I. Identify the objects that are shaped like a sphere. Mark an X on those objects.

176

Lesson 89

COMMON CORE STANDARD CC.K.G.2

Lesson Objective: Identify, name, and describe three-dimensional shapes including cubes.

Identify, Name, and Describe Cubes

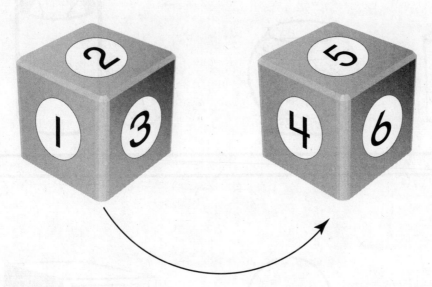

_____

- - - - - -

_____ **flat surfaces**

DIRECTIONS 1. Look at the pictures that show all the flat surfaces on one cube. Count how many flat surfaces. Touch each number as you count. 2. Write the number that shows how many flat surfaces.

Geometry

Identify, Name, and Describe Cubes

DIRECTIONS I. Identify the objects that are shaped like a cube. Mark an X on those objects.

Identify, Name, and Describe Cylinders

 1

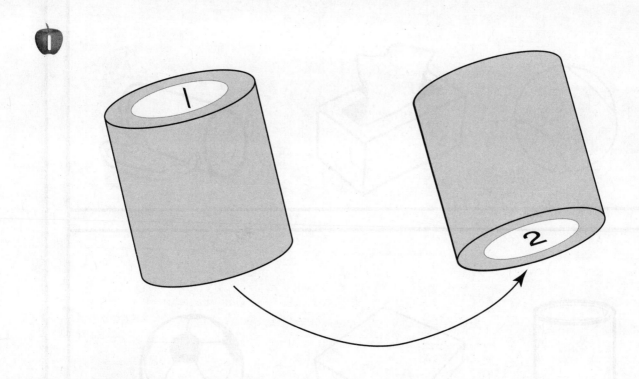

2

_____

- - - - - - - -

_____ **flat surfaces**

DIRECTIONS **1.** Look at the pictures that show the flat surfaces on one cylinder. Count how many flat surfaces. Touch each number as you count. **2.** Write the number that shows how many flat surfaces.

Geometry

Identify, Name, and Describe Cylinders

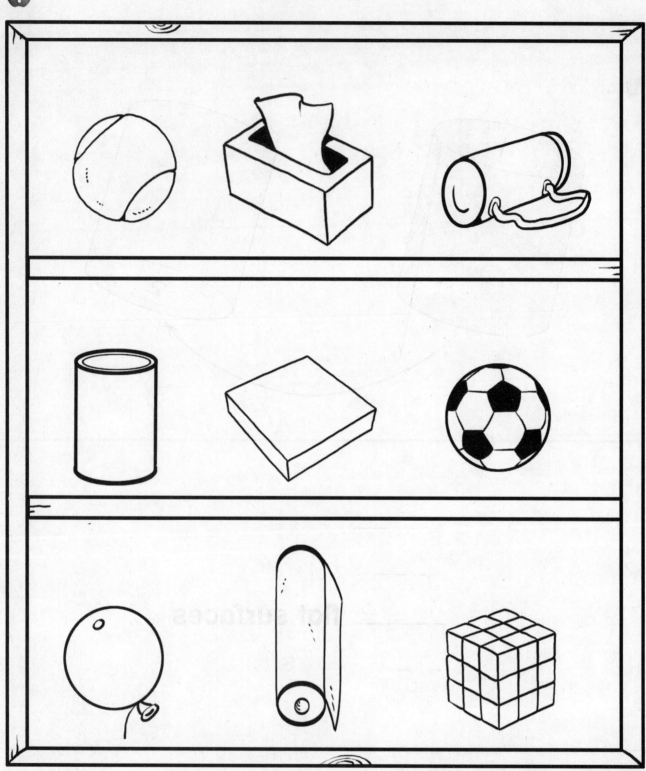

DIRECTIONS **1.** Identify the objects that are shaped like a cylinder. Mark an X on those objects.

Identify, Name, and Describe Cones

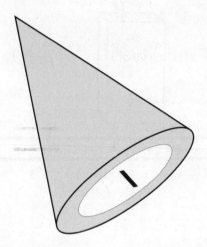

_____

_ _ _ _ _ _ _

_____ **flat surface**

DIRECTIONS **1.** Look at the picture that shows the flat surface on one cone. Count how many flat surfaces. Touch the number as you count. **2.** Write the number that shows how many flat surfaces.

Geometry

Identify, Name, and Describe Cones

DIRECTIONS **I.** Identify the objects that are shaped like a cone. Mark an X on those objects.

Problem Solving • Two- and Three-Dimensional Shapes

1

red

blue

2

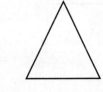

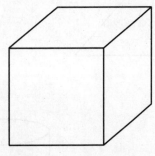

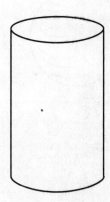

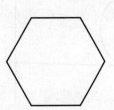

DIRECTIONS **1.** Use red to color the two-dimensional or flat shape. Use blue to color the three-dimensional or solid shape. **2.** Look at the shape you colored red in Exercise 1. Use red to color the flat shapes. Look at the shape you colored blue in Exercise 1. Use blue to color the solid shapes.

Geometry

Name _____

Problem Solving • Two- and Three-Dimensional Shapes

 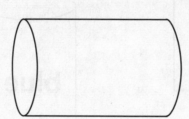 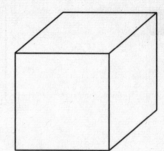

 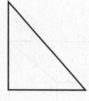 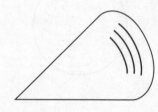

 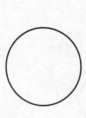 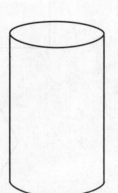 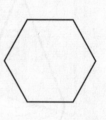

DIRECTIONS   1. Identify the two-dimensional or flat shapes. Use red to color the flat shapes. Identify the three-dimensional or solid shapes. Use blue to color the solid shapes.

Describe Circles

COMMON CORE STANDARD CC.K.G.4
Lesson Objective: Describe attributes of circles.

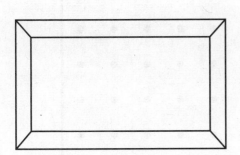 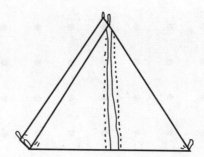 

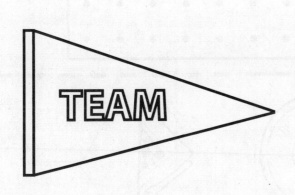 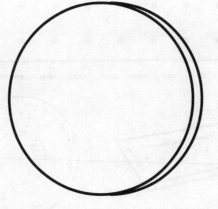 

DIRECTIONS   **I.** Finish coloring the object that is shaped like a circle.   **2.** Color the object that is shaped like a circle.

Describe Circles

 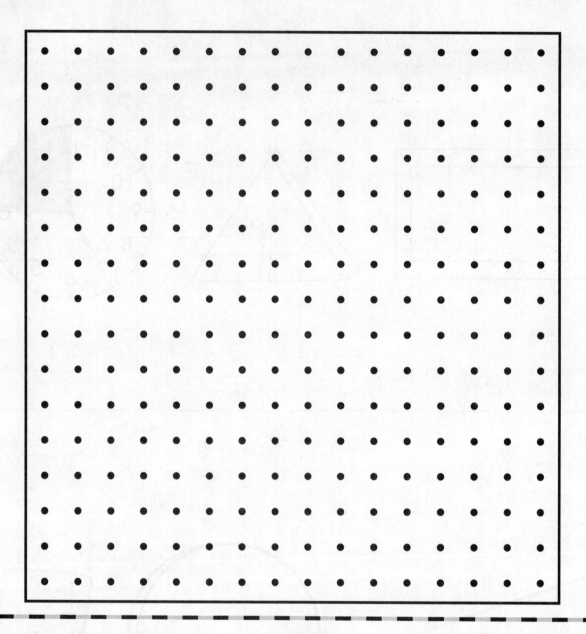

 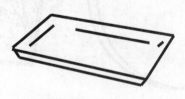 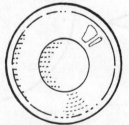 

DIRECTIONS 1. Use a pencil to hold one end of a large paper clip on one of the dots in the center. Place another pencil in the other end of the paper clip. Move the pencil around to draw a circle. 2. Color the object that is shaped like a circle.

Name _____

Lesson 94
COMMON CORE STANDARD CC.K.G.4
Lesson Objective: Describe attributes of squares.

Describe Squares

 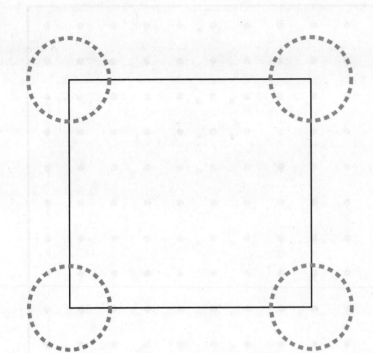

_____

- - - - - - - - -

_____ **vertices**

 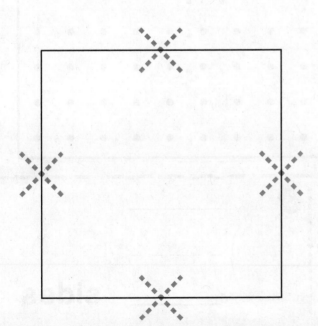

_____

- - - - - - - - -

_____ **sides**

DIRECTIONS **1.** Trace the circle around each corner, or vertex. Draw a dot in each circle as you count. Write how many corners, or vertices. **2.** Trace the X on each side. Draw a dot on each X as you count. Write how many sides.

Geometry

Name _____

Describe Squares

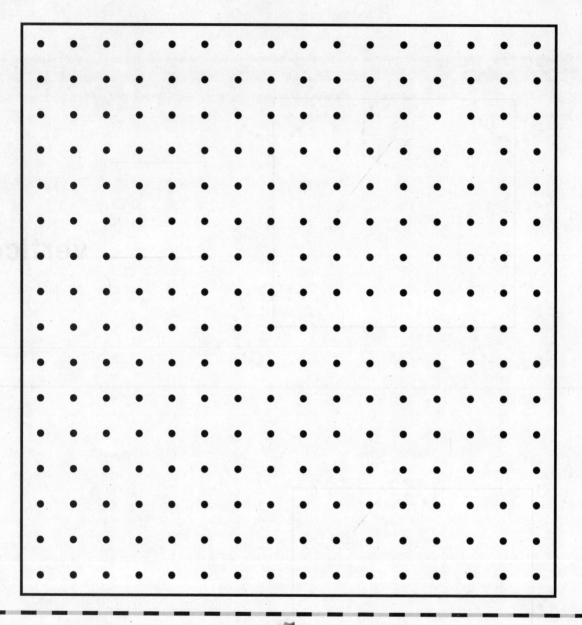

_____ **vertices**   _____ **sides**

DIRECTIONS **1.** Draw and color a square.   **2.** Place a counter on each corner, or vertex, of the square that you drew. Write how many corners, or vertices.   **3.** Trace around the sides of the square that you drew. Write how many sides.

Name _____

Describe Triangles

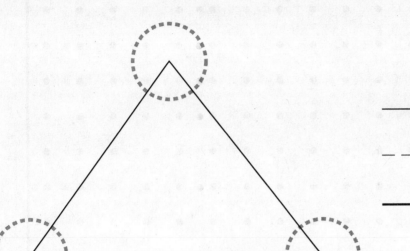

_____

- - - - - - - -

_____ **vertices**

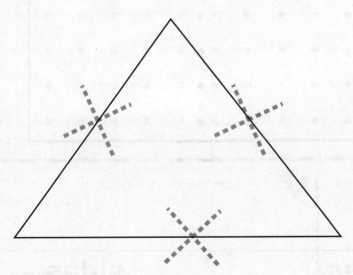

_____

- - - - - - - -

_____ **sides**

DIRECTIONS **I.** Trace the circle around each corner, or vertex. Draw a dot in each circle as you count. Write how many corners, or vertices. **2.** Trace the X on each side. Draw a dot on each X as you count. Write how many sides.

Geometry

Describe Triangles

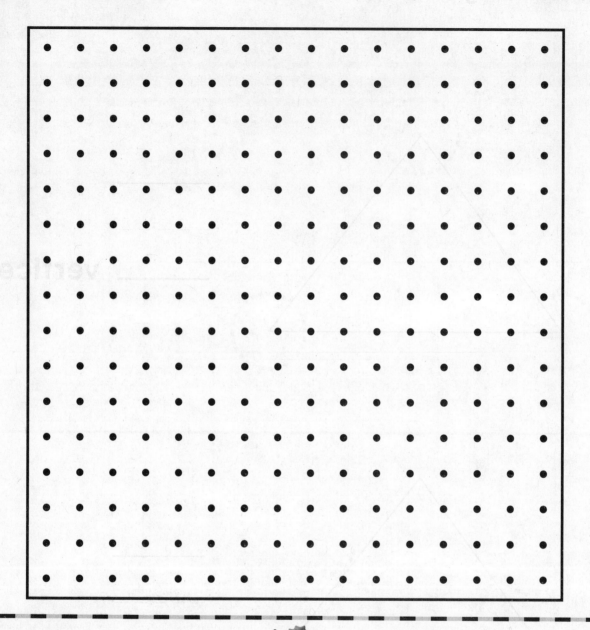

_ _ _ _ _ _ _ _ _ _ _ _ _ _ _

_____ **vertices**   _____ **sides**

DIRECTIONS I. Draw and color a triangle. 2. Place a counter on each corner, or vertex, of the triangle that you drew. Write how many corners, or vertices. 3. Trace around the sides of the triangle that you drew. Write how many sides.

Name _____

Lesson 96
COMMON CORE STANDARD CC.K.G.4
Lesson Objective: Describe attributes of rectangles.

Describe Rectangles

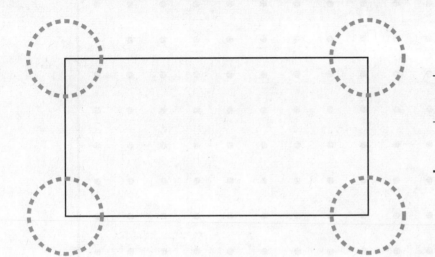

_____

- - - - - - - - - -

_____ **vertices**

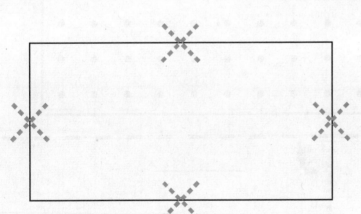

_____

- - - - - - - - - -

_____ **sides**

DIRECTIONS **1.** Trace the circle around each corner, or vertex. Draw a dot in each circle as you count. Write how many corners, or vertices. **2.** Trace the X on each side. Draw a dot on each X as you count. Write how many sides.

Geometry

Describe Rectangles

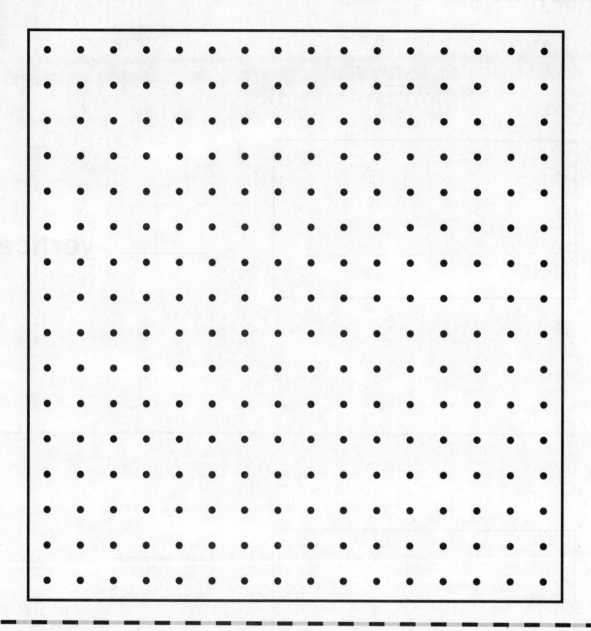

2 _____
         - - - - -
         _____ **vertices**

3 _____
         - - - - -
         _____ **sides**

DIRECTIONS 1. Draw and color a rectangle. **2.** Place a counter on each corner, or vertex, of the rectangle that you drew. Write how many corners, or vertices. **3.** Trace around the sides of the rectangle that you drew. Write how many sides.

Lesson 97

COMMON CORE STANDARD CC.K.G.4
Lesson Objective: Describe attributes of hexagons.

Describe Hexagons

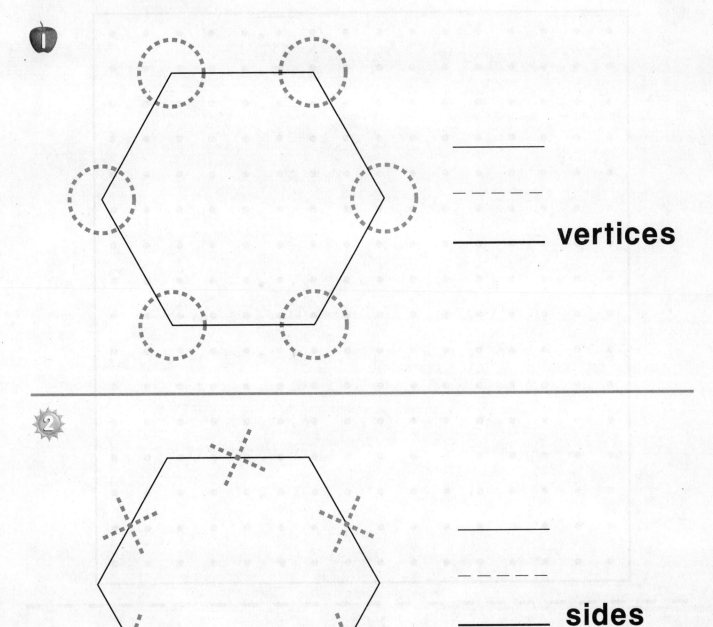

vertices

sides

DIRECTIONS 1. Trace the circle around each corner, or vertex. Draw a dot in each circle as you count. Write how many corners, or vertices. 2. Trace the X on each side. Draw a dot on each X as you count. Write how many sides.

Geometry

Name _____

Describe Hexagons

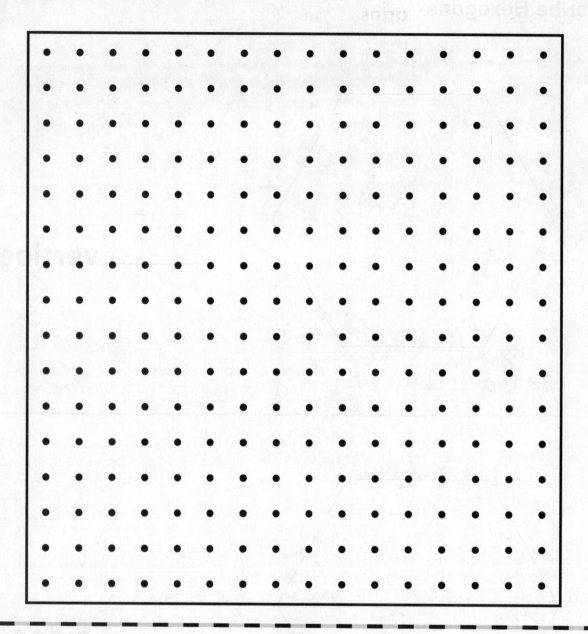

_____ **vertices**   _____ **sides**

DIRECTIONS **1.** Draw and color a hexagon. **2.** Place a counter on each corner, or vertex, of the hexagon that you drew. Write how many corners, or vertices. **3.** Trace around the sides of the hexagon that you drew. Write how many sides.

194

Lesson 98

COMMON CORE STANDARD CC.K.G.4

Lesson Objective: Use the words *alike* and *different* to compare two-dimensional shapes by attributes.

Algebra • Compare
Two-Dimensional Shapes

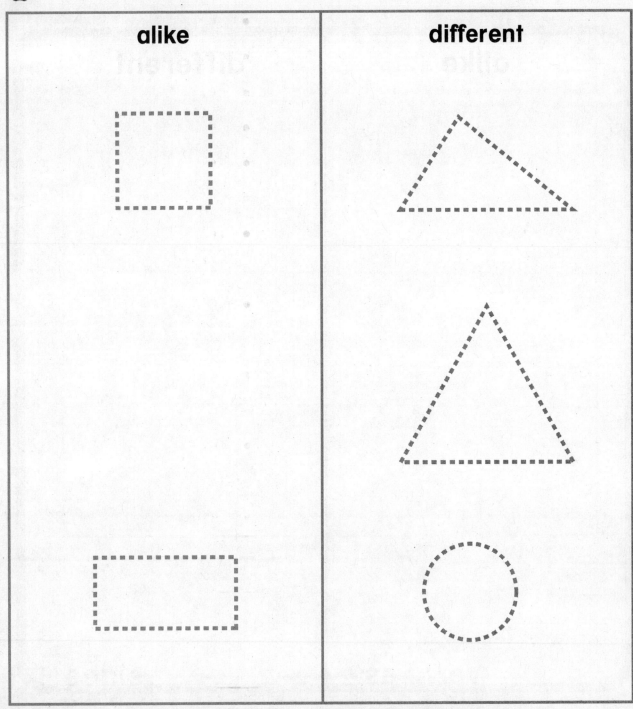

DIRECTIONS **I.** Sort two-dimensional shapes by number of vertices as shown.
Trace the shapes that have four vertices. Tell a friend why the shapes are alike.
Trace the other shapes. Tell a friend why they are different.

Geometry

Algebra • Compare
Two-Dimensional Shapes

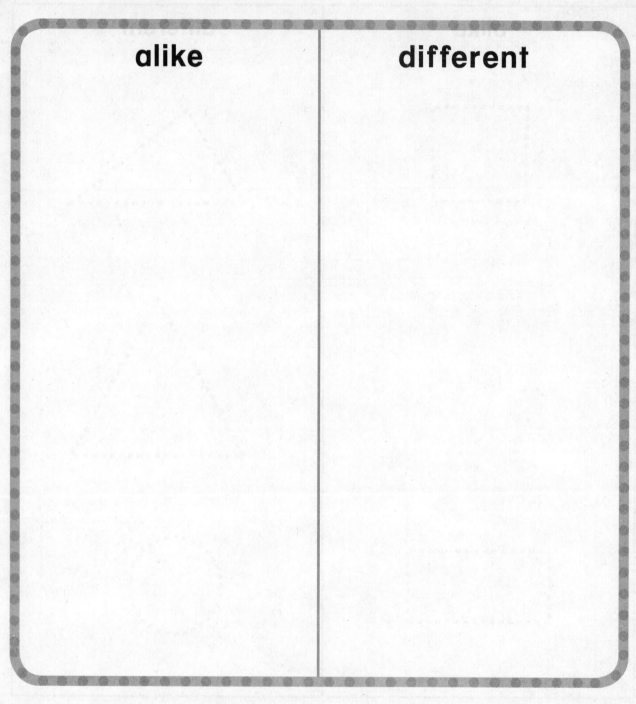

alike	different

DIRECTIONS 1. Place two-dimensional shapes on the page. Sort the shapes by the number of sides. Draw the shapes on the sorting mat. Use the words *alike* and *different* to tell how you sorted the shapes.

196

Name _____

Lesson 99
COMMON CORE STANDARD CC.K.G.4
Lesson Objective: Analyze and compare three-dimensional shapes by attributes.

Three-Dimensional Shapes

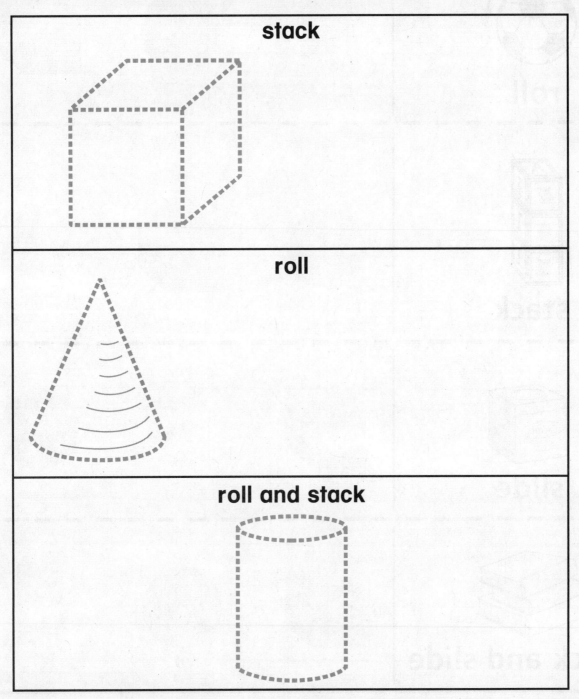

DIRECTIONS I. Place three-dimensional shapes on the page. Sort the shapes by whether they roll or stack. Describe the shapes. Match a picture of each shape to the shapes. Glue the shape pictures on the page.

Geometry

Three-Dimensional Shapes

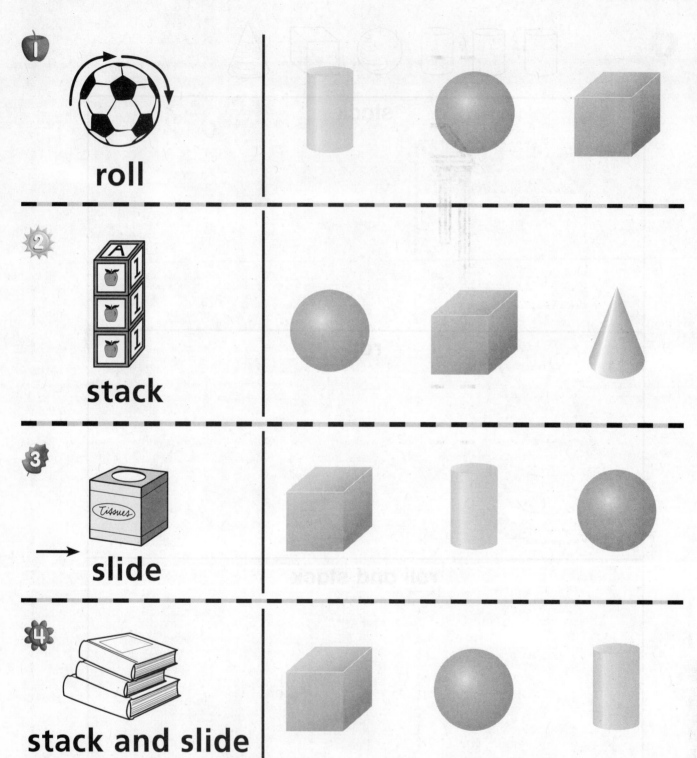

roll

stack

slide

stack and slide

DIRECTIONS 1. Which shape does not roll? Mark an X on that shape. 2. Which shapes do not stack? Mark an X on those shapes. 3. Which shape does not slide? Mark an X on that shape. 4. Which shape does not stack and slide? Mark an X on that shape.

Build Models

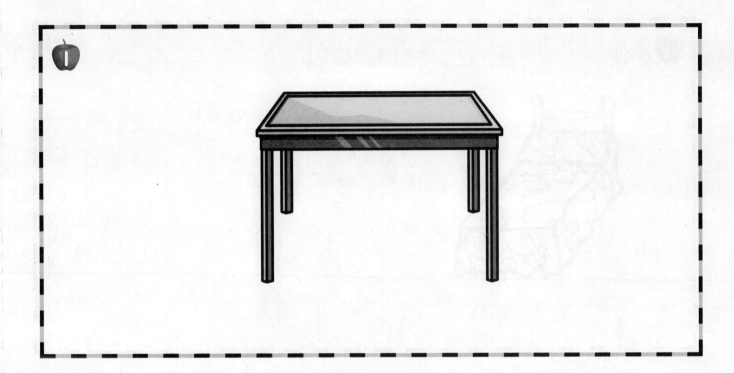

DIRECTIONS I–2. Make a model of the object with blocks.

Geometry

Build Models

 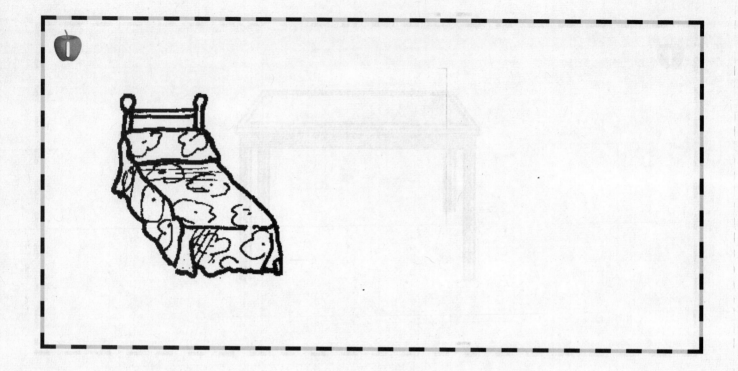

DIRECTIONS Make a model of the object with blocks.

Make Shapes

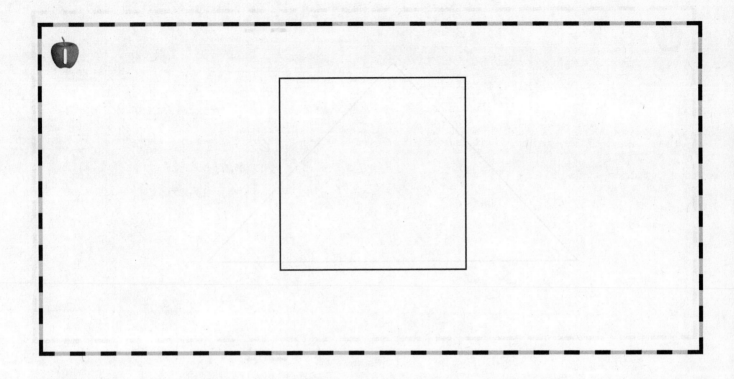

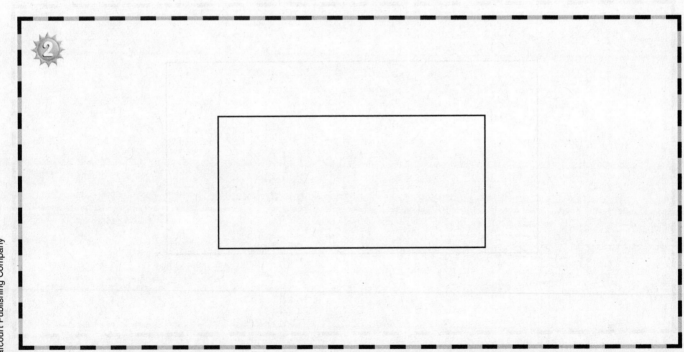

DIRECTIONS   1–2. Make the shape with triangles.
Then trace the shapes you used.

Geometry

Make Shapes

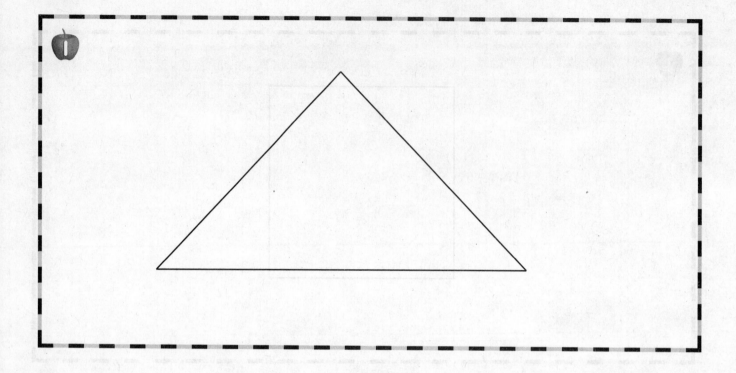

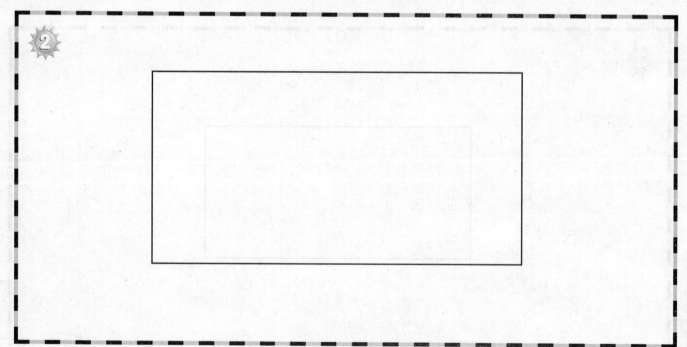

DIRECTIONS Make the shape with triangles. Then trace the shapes you used.

Problem Solving • Draw to Join Shapes

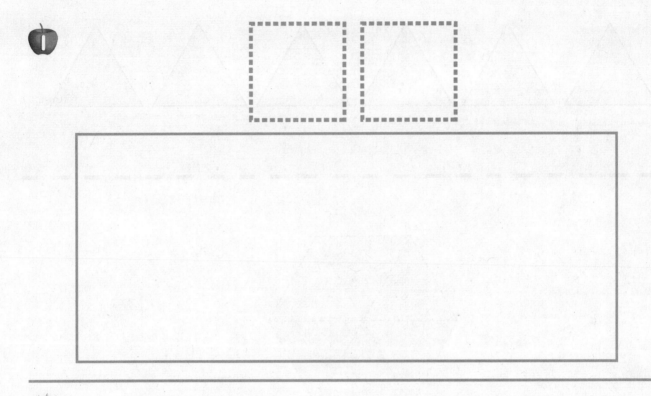

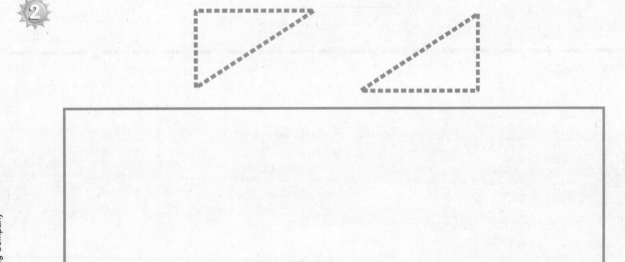

DIRECTIONS Place two-dimensional shapes on the page as shown. **I.** How can you use the two squares to make a rectangle? Trace around the squares to draw the rectangle. **2.** How can you use the two triangles to make a rectangle? Trace around the triangles to draw the rectangle.

Geometry

Problem Solving • Draw to Join Shapes

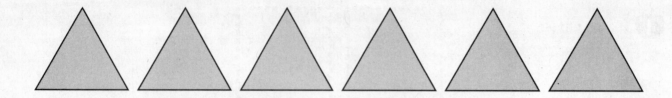

 1

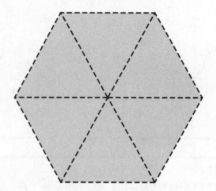

2

© Houghton Mifflin Harcourt Publishing Company

DIRECTIONS **I.** Place triangles on the page as shown. How can you join all
of the triangles to make a hexagon? Trace around the triangles to draw the hexagon.
2. How can you join some of the triangles to make a larger triangle? Trace around the
triangles to draw the larger triangle.